Brexit and Aviation Law

T0316343

Focusing on the consequences of Brexit for aviation law, this book presents the key legal issues for aviation business and administration, as well as all major stakeholders that could potentially be affected by Brexit. This will include airlines, airports, aerospace manufacturers, regulatory and judicial institutions, passengers and employees. The book will indicate groups of legal acts disturbed by Brexit and those few that will remain untouched, and develop on this basis a digest of regulatory and institutional problems that will arise in various areas of the discussed sector. Finally, the short title will deliberate on the directions of possible actions which may be undertaken 'o avoid post-Brexit legal incoherence. This review should give essential uidance to the industry and the authorities on both sides of the English nannel as to what to expect and how to prepare for the forthcoming legal hquake.

Valulik, PhD is head of the Civil Aviation Laboratory at the Centre itrust and Regulatory Studies, Faculty of Management, University aw, and an attorney practising in commercial and corporate law. He tures in air law at the Warsaw School of Economics, Poland.

Legal Perspectives on Brexit
Series Editor:
Richard Lang (University of Brighton, UK)
Editorial Board:
David Edward CMG, QC, MA, LLB, LLD, FRSE (University
of Edinburgh, UK, Emeritus)
Margot Horspool (University of Surrey, UK, Emeritus)
Shirley McDonagh (CILEx, UK)

'Legal Perspectives on Brexit' is a peer-reviewed series of shortform books
which goes beyond responding to public curiosity aroused by the trigger-
ing of Article 50 to recognise the ongoing legal and political disputes Brexit
has prompted. Aimed at academics and professionals it provides expert
commentary on and predictions about the possible legislative and judicial
implications of Brexit for each of the different sectors of regulation which
have for so long been dominated by EU Law, creating a valuable one stop
resource which exposes, explores and perhaps even resolves legal problems
stemming from the separation of UK and EU legal systems.

www.routledge.com/law/series/BREXIT

Brexit and Aviation Law
Jan Walulik

Forthcoming

Brexit and Procurement Law
Catherine Maddox

Brexit, the NHS and Health Law
Jean McHale

Brexit and Energy Law
Raphael Heffron

Brexit and Aviation Law

Jan Walulik

Routledge
Taylor & Francis Group

LONDON AND NEW YORK

First published 2019 by Routledge

2 Park Square, Milton Park, Abingdon, Oxfordshire OX14 4RN

52 Vanderbilt Avenue, New York, NY 10017

Routledge is an imprint of the Taylor & Francis Group, an informa business

First issued in paperback 2020

British Library Cataloguing-in-Publication Data
A catalogue record for this book is available from the British Library

Library of Congress Cataloging-in-Publication Data
Names: Walulik, Jan, author.
Title: Brexit and aviation law / Jan Walulik.
Description: Abingdon, Oxon ; New York, NY : Routledge, 2019. |
    Series: Legal perspectives on Brexit | Includes bibliographical
    references and index.
Identifiers: LCCN 2018040165 | ISBN 9781138591370 (hbk)
Subjects: LCSH: Aeronautics, Commercial—Law and
    legislation—Great Britain. | Aeronautics, Commercial—Law
    and legislation—European Union countries. | International and
    municipal law—Great Britain. | European Union—Great Britain.
Classification: LCC KD2732 .W35 2019 | DDC 343.4109/7—dc23
LC record available at https://lccn.loc.gov/2018040165

ISBN: 978-1-138-59137-0 (hbk)
ISBN: 978-0-367-60657-2 (pbk)

Typeset in Times New Roman
by Apex CoVantage, LLC

Contents

Appendix

Summary dashboard

Red: urgent issues to resolve

- A huge part of the UK's international aviation relations will be disturbed, leading to loss of traffic rights.
- Need for simultaneous negotiation and completion of aviation deals with a vast number of states.
- Reliance on comity and reciprocity possible, but unstable – not viable long term.
- Current EU aviation regime or EU-third party aviation regimes: the UK will generally have to make new arrangements with foreign partners.
- Member states' horizontally amended bilateral agreements: the UK will not be considered an EU member state referred to in horizontal agreements, even in its own bilateral agreements. Need to renegotiate.
- UK bilateral agreements containing EU ownership and control clauses: in such cases, the UK-based airlines (i.e. holding British Air Operator Certificates) will cease to be EU air carriers as referred to in these clauses and, notwithstanding their ownership and control structure, will not be eligible for designation by the UK.
- EU aviation safety, security and Single European Sky systems: the UK will need to duplicate this regulatory legacy or remain part of these systems. The former choice would be time and resource consuming. The latter would require a new aviation arrangement with the EU, including UK's participation in the European Aviation Safety Agency.
- Need to negotiate new instruments to replace e.g. agreements on aviation safety (reciprocal acceptance of approvals) and security (one-stop security) entered into by the EU pursuant to its competences, which will not apply to the UK after Brexit.

- Possible loss of passenger rights (EU compensation rules, expanded application of Montreal Convention).
- Need to improve long-haul hubs if relations with third parties are to be developed.

Amber: minor issues to resolve

- The European Union (Withdrawal) Act will provide for domestication of EU law. Most of the retained laws will require important adjustments to become operative.
- EU Passenger Name Record rules will cease to apply to and in the UK: UK henceforward will be free to make its own rules below or above the current level of data protection, taking into account the need/ desire for future exchange arrangements with EU27 member states and/or third countries.
- The UK will be outside EU environment protection laws. This may lead to some conflicts with the EU.
- The UK will have to reconsider its declarations/commitments under Cape Town Convention and GATS.
- UK participation in EU aerospace programmes will require new arrangements.

Green: staying the same

- Some international aviation treaties and agreements to which the UK is a party, e.g. the ICAO framework, the EUROCONTROL framework, the Warsaw-Montreal system and the Tokyo-Hague-Montreal system will not be disturbed by Brexit.
- Any contract wherein the parties have chosen English law as the governing law (e.g. wet lease agreements, dry lease agreements) should not be disturbed at least as far as choice of law is concerned (although nota bene enforceability).

Glossary

AOC	air operator certificate
CAA	Common Aviation Area
CJEU	Court of Justice (EU), previously Court of Justice of the European Communities
CRS	computer reservation systems
EASA	EU Aviation Safety Agency, previously European Aviation Safety Agency
ECA	European Communities Act 1972
ECAC	European Civil Aviation Conference
ECAA	European Common Aviation Area
EEA	the European Economic Area
EFTA	European Free Trade Association
EU	European Union (previously European Community, European Economic Community)
EU27	European Union without the UK
GATS	General Agreement on Trade in Services
LCC	low-cost carrier
PNR	passenger name record
REIO	regional economic integration organisation
SES	Single European Sky
TEU	Treaty on the European Union
TFEU	Treaty – Treaty on the Functioning of the European Union
Treaties	TEU and TFEU
UK	United Kingdom
VCLT	Vienna Convention on the Law of Treaties
WTO	World Trade Organization

Introduction

Following the referendum of 23 June 2016, London has triggered the procedure for the UK's departure from the EU. On 29 March 2017, the British Prime Minister submitted to the European Council the notice of withdrawal subject to Article 50(2) of the Treaty on the European Union (TEU).[1] The European Council has issued its guidelines on Brexit in line with Article 50(2) TEU, and the negotiations of an agreement setting out the arrangements for the UK's withdrawal ('Withdrawal Agreement') have commenced. On 19 March 2018, a Draft Withdrawal Agreement was published, providing among other things for a so-called transition period – regarded as a *status quo* arrangement – to end on 31 December 2020.[2] From the legal standpoint the British notice means that, unless otherwise decided in the final Withdrawal Agreement, EU treaty law and derived law will cease to apply to Britain from 30 March 2019, 00:00 Central European Time (29 March 2019, 23:00 Greenwich Mean Time), and the UK will cease to be a member of the EU from that date ('Exit Day'). From the practical standpoint, it means that the UK will have to re-establish its competences in all issues governed by the EU and will need to define its future relations with the diminished EU consisting of 27 member states ('EU27').

This will not be a smooth process, and not surprisingly, analysts point to economic slowdown following Brexit.[3] In the aviation sector, given the size of the UK's market and its role in Europe, it will be especially hard to provide for an open, coherent and transparent post-Brexit market

---

1 Treaty on the European Union, done at Maastricht on 7 February 1992, consolidated version [2016] OJ C202/13, entered into force on 1 November 1993.

2 Draft Withdrawal Agreement of 19 March 2018, TF50 (2018) 35. At the time of writing, there is still a lot to be finalised, and, of course, negotiations could still break up with no final agreement at all. For the transition period, see Chapter 17 of this book.

3 E.g.: R Kierzenkowski and others, 'The Economic Consequences of Brexit. A Taxing Decision' (OECD Economic Policy Paper No 16, 2016).

environment. The UK represents the largest aviation market in the EU and the third largest in the world. There are approximately 3,000 departures from UK airports every day,[4] and these airports account for 17.7% of the total passenger traffic handled by EU airports (256.4 million passengers at UK airports out of 1.448 billion passengers at EU airports).[5] Aviation is key to the UK's connectivity with nearly three-quarters of visitors to the UK and 40% of the UK's trade by value travelling by air.[6]

There is a high level of dependence of the UK aviation sector on the EU27 aviation markets, with the EU27 being single biggest destination market for the UK, accounting for 49% of passengers and 54% of scheduled commercial flights.[7] The average share of passengers handled by EU27 airports flying to and from the UK is only 11.5%. However, the reliance of particular EU27 countries and airports on the UK market may be much greater.[8] UK-EU27 air traffic has a significant direct, indirect and induced economic impact. According to ACI Europe estimates, this traffic supports 285,000 jobs and is associated with EUR 13.7 billion GDP in the EU27. At the same time, it gives rise to 270,000 jobs and contributes to EUR 15.4 billion GDP in the UK.[9] UK-EU27 economic integration in aviation is magnified by cross-border ownership (e.g. IAG) and advanced operations performed by air carriers outside their home states (e.g. Ryanair, easyJet). The high level of interdependence between the UK and EU27 is also noticeable in aerospace manufacturing where trans-border projects, production and investments are part of everyday business.

Against these realities, it is clear that the UK's withdrawal from the EU will have a tremendous impact on aviation activities. Although post-Brexit macroeconomic conditions will also disturb this sector, the discussed impact will generally come from a major shift in the regulatory framework. Consequently, the aim of this book will be to investigate the exact impact

4 P McClean and A Barker, 'UK airlines brought down to earth by Brexit' *Financial Times* (London, 13 February 2017) 5.
5 Airports Council International Europe, 'Brexit & Aviation. Market Interdependence and Economic Value' (ACI Europe 2017) 1.
6 See 'New Aviation Agreements to Underpin a Truly Global Britain' (Airport Operators Association, 17 January 2017) <www.aoa.org.uk/2017/01/new-aviation-agreements-to-underpin-a-truly-global-britain/> accessed 3 May 2018.
7 International Air Transport Association, *The Impact of 'BREXIT' on UK Air Transport* (IATA Economics 2016) 4.
8 See J Wiltshire, 'An Economic View on Political Developments: Implications for Aviation' (Brexit: The Legal & Operational Implications, Royal Aeronautical Society Seminar, London, January 2017); Airports Council International Europe (n 5) 2–4.
9 Ibid 5.

of Brexit on particular parts of aviation law and to suggest how the UK's withdrawal from the EU may be managed from this perspective.

Part I of the book will reveal groups of legal acts that will be hit by Brexit and those which will be intact. Discussed will be the exact impact of Brexit on legal instruments and on their application in and to the UK, as well as on the UK's relations with EU27 and third states. Part II will explain how the post-Brexit changes in the legal framework will work on regulatory content concerning key aviation activities. The following Part III will show the corresponding impact on institutions and proceedings. These chapters will generally present a scenario whereby no post-Brexit solutions are adopted as regards the discussed matters ('hard Brexit'). Possible measures will only be mentioned where necessary and will be discussed in detail in relation to the UK-EU27, UK domestic and UK-third party fora in Part IV of the book.[10]

---

10 This will be based on the state of statute books and UK-EU27 negotiation documents valid as of the end of September 2018.

Part I

Impact of Brexit on groups of legal acts

Aviation activity in the EU and in the UK is ruled by thousands of legal acts. These acts, that are instituted at the national, EU and international multilateral levels, set up various regulatory systems. The aim of this part of the book is to indicate groups of legal acts the application of which will be distressed by Brexit and those which will survive Brexit. The following chapters will present the consequences of a hard Brexit; that is a situation whereby no deal is reached before Exit Day between the UK and EU27 or between the UK and third parties as to the application of particular aviation laws. The role of British legislation adopted to address post-Brexit issues will only be mentioned in brief.[1] This part will also leave aside a possible transition period when the discussed instruments could continue to be applied *mutatis mutandis* after Brexit.[2]

It is important to note that aviation laws have been very widely harmonised at the EU level. Therefore, the acts that will be touched by Brexit constitute a major part of air law applicable to and in the UK. Due to the exit from the EU, new legal measures will have to be taken by British lawmakers. Given the scope of regulation covered by the affected instruments, this task will be absolutely tremendous, and it is doubtful whether the UK will be able to manage it in a short timescale. The impact on legal acts will also be huge in economic terms, since Brexit will erase the legal basis for most current UK air traffic.

---

1 Post-Brexit measures will be presented in detail in Part IV of this book.
2 For the transition period, see Chapter 17 of this book.

1   Brexit-affected legal acts

This chapter will point to groups of legal acts that will be upset by Brexit. In most cases, the impact of Brexit will mean that specific pieces of law will cease to apply to and/or in the UK, to UK-EU relations or to UK-third party relations. This may result in legal gaps, in changes in relations between legal acts, or possibly in revival of some legal acts over which EU law currently prevails. In some instances, Brexit will only have a partial impact on existing laws and will require additional actions from the UK.

1.1 EU primary law

The EU primary (treaty) law comprises several international agreements of which the main two, known as the founding treaties, are the TEU and the Treaty on the Functioning of the European Union (TFEU, the Treaty),[1] also referred to as 'the Treaties'. These acts are a key part of the legislative framework relating to Brexit. The former includes the legal basis for the withdrawal from the EU, whereas the latter is base for the EU single air market.

Initially, European law did not cover air transport regulation. Before the liberalisation process started, air transport within the EU states was subject to domestic regulations, whereas air transport between these states was governed by bilateral agreements which were concluded within the framework of the Chicago Convention.[2] Part III Title VI TFEU (Articles 90–100)[3] has always contained common rules for transport. However, according to Article

---

1 Treaty on the Functioning of the European Union, signed on 25 March 1957 in Rome, entered into force on 1 January 1958 (then Treaty establishing the European Economic Community [TEEC], later Treaty establishing the European Community [TEC]), consolidated version [2016] OJ C202/47.
2 Convention on International Civil Aviation, signed at Chicago on 7 September 1944, ICAO Doc 7300/9; UNTS, Vol. 15, No 295, entered into force on 30 January 1945. For the scope of the Chicago-bilateral system see also Chapter 2.1 of this book.
3 Ex Part III Title V TEC (Articles 70–80), ex Part III Title IV TEEC (Articles 74–84).

100(2) TFEU,[4] the application of provisions regarding common transport policy set forth in this title was subject to the decision of the Council.

It was not until the late 1980s that the EU[5] decided to incorporate aviation into its common transport policy, and to unify the air transport industries of its member states within a single air market. The impulse came from the application of another part of the Treaty to the air transport sector. In 1986, the Court of Justice (CJEU) ruled, in the *Nouvelles Frontiéres* case, that despite the lack of sectorial competition rules regarding air transport, the respective Treaty rules included in Part III Title VII Chapter 1 Section 1 (Articles 101–106)[6] shall apply directly to competition in air transport.[7] This encouraged the adoption of competition rules and a common transport policy in the airline sector. Under the Single European Act,[8] the EU was finally obliged to take this initiative and to establish a single market, including a single air market, by the end of 1992.

This harmonisation has been achieved by derived law.[9] However, the foundation stone of EU air law has always been in the Treaty principles concerning transport policy and competition. The TFEU provisions on transport policy envisage the adoption of common rules applicable to intra-EU trans-border and domestic transport and of measures to improve transport safety and other appropriate provisions. They also embrace instructions as to public aids, transport rates and conditions, prohibited discrimination and protectionism. The Treaty competition rules established in Title VII Chapter 1 outline the prohibited anticompetitive actions, abuse of dominant position and state aids distorting competition which are deemed to be incompatible with the internal market. Equally important for the functioning of EU air transport are the free movement of goods (Title II TFEU) and the free movement of persons, services and capital (Title IV TFEU).

Currently, the described constitution of the EU single air market applies in the territories of the EU member states including the UK (Article 52 TEU) and in those European territories for whose external relations an EU member state is responsible (Article 355[3] TFEU), which includes Gibraltar.[10] Subject to special arrangements for association set out in Part Four

---

4 Ex Article 80(2) TEC, ex Article 84(2) TEEC.
5 Then the European Community.
6 Then Part III Title V Chapter 1 TEEC (Articles 85–90).
7 Judgment of the Court of 30 April 1986: Cases C-209–213/84 *Ministère Public v Lucas Asjes and Others* [1986] ECR 1425.
8 The Single European Act, signed at Luxembourg on 17 February 1986 and at The Hague on 28 February 1986 [1987] OJ L169/1, entered into force on 1 July 1987.
9 See Chapter 1.2 of this book.
10 However, according to the declaration by Spain and the UK, the application of the Treaties to Gibraltar shall not imply changes in the respective positions of the member states concerned.

of the TFEU, the Treaties shall partially apply to some overseas countries and territories.[11] The applicable rules of EU primary law can be relied on directly by individuals before EU member states' courts.

The previously mentioned Treaty rules which are relevant for the EU single air market will cease to apply to the UK, its overseas and European territories and to UK-EU27 relations on Exit Day. Article 50(3) TEU states explicitly that the Treaties shall cease to apply to the withdrawing state from the date of entry into force of the withdrawal agreement or, failing that, two years after the notification of the intention of withdrawal, unless the Council, in agreement with the member state concerned, unanimously decides to prolong this period. It is, however, unclear if and to what extent the Treaties will cease to apply to Gibraltar airport after Brexit.[12]

1.2 EU-derived law

Although the fundamental principles of EU transport policy arise from the TFEU, the core of EU air law consists in derived law, also known as the *acquis communautaire*, including hundreds of regulations and directives constituting the European single air market. These acts govern a predominant part of civil aviation activity in the EU. The European single air market was built up in three phases. At the end of 1987, the Council issued a package of four acts (the I liberalisation package)[13] which liberalised the criteria of tariff regulation and allowed member states' carriers to operate services

11 This includes British overseas territories listed in Annex II to the TFEU.
12 The same problem arises in the context of pieces of EU derived law, and EU-third party agreements. These acts include a reservation that their application is understood to be without prejudice to the respective legal positions of Spain and the UK with regard to the dispute over sovereignty over the territory in which the airport is situated. The provisions of the Draft Agreement on the withdrawal of the United Kingdom of Great Britain and Northern Ireland from the European Union and the European Atomic Energy Community (Draft Withdrawal Agreement) of 19 March 2018, TF50 (2018) refer directly to these arrangements. Article 3(1)(b) of this draft agreement states that any reference in this agreement to the UK or its territory, shall be understood as referring to Gibraltar to the extent that EU law was applicable to it before the date of entry into force of this agreement. See also Chapter 17 of this book.
13 Council Regulation (EEC) No 3975/87 of 14 December 1987 laying down the procedure for the application of the rules on competition to undertakings in the air transport sector [1987] OJ L374/1; Council Regulation (EEC) No 3976/87 of 14 December 1987 on the application of Article 85 (3) of the Treaty to certain categories of agreements and concerted practices in the air transport sector [1987] OJ L374/9; Council Directive (EEC) No 87/601 of 14 December 1987 on fares for scheduled air services between member states [1987] OJ L374/12; Council Decision (EEC) No 87/602 of 14 December 1987 on the sharing of passenger capacity between air carriers on scheduled air services between member states and on access for air carriers to scheduled air-service routes between member states [1987] OJ L374/19.

embracing the Third and Fourth Freedoms of the Air[14] within interregional EU routes. These regulations were superseded in 1990 by the II package,[15] which brought about further liberalisation as regards air carrier designation, tariffs, route authorities and capacity in regular air services. In 1991, tariffs were deregulated and the Third, Fourth and Fifth Freedoms of the Air were introduced for air post and air cargo services within the EU.[16] Finally, full liberalisation was instituted by the III package of 1992.[17] This set of laws, which came into force on 1 January 1993, established a single community air market, harmonised market access rules, entirely liberalised route rights, and unified rules for regular and irregular air services within the EU. It also liberalised cabotage services starting from 1 April 1997. The regulations on market access and tariffs have been revised and reconfirmed in current EU regulation 1008/2008.[18]

The derived law concerning air transport has united member states' air markets and established a system of economic regulation based on freedom of services (free routes, tariffs and capacity determination) within the EU. It has also harmonised air carrier licensing and has replaced the airline national ownership and control requirements with an EU ownership and control standard. Each airline having a valid EU license may now operate any air service within the EU without the need to obtain permission from

---

14 For Freedoms of the Air, see Chapter 2.1 of this book.

15 Council Regulation (EEC) No 2342/90 of 24 July 1990 on fares for scheduled air services [1990] OJ L217/1; Council Regulation (EEC) No 2343/90 of 24 July 1990 on access for air carriers to scheduled intra-Community air service routes and on the sharing of passenger capacity between air carriers on scheduled air services between member states [1990] OJ L217/8; Council Regulation (EEC) No 2344/90 of 24 July 1990 amending Regulation (EEC) No 3976/87 on the application of article 85(3) of the Treaty to certain categories of agreements and concerted practices in the air transport sector [1990] OJ L217/15.

16 Council Regulation (EEC) No 294/91 of 4 February 1991 on the operation of air cargo services between member states [1991] OJ L36/1.

17 Council Regulation (EEC) No 2407/92 of 23 July 1992 on licensing of air carriers [1992] OJ L240/1; Council Regulation (EEC) No 2408/92 of 23 July 1992 on access for Community air carriers to intra-Community air routes [1992] OJ L240/8; Council Regulation (EEC) No 2409/92 of 23 July 1992 on fares and rates for air services [1992] OJ L240/15; Council Regulation (EEC) No 2410/92 of 23 July 1992 amending Regulation (EEC) No 3975/87 laying down the procedure for the application of the rules on competition to undertakings in the air transport sector [1992] OJ L240/18; Council Regulation (EEC) No 2411/92 of 23 July 1992 amending Regulation (EEC) No 3976/87 on the application of Article 85(3) of the Treaty to certain categories of agreements and concerted practices in the air transport sector [1992] OJ L240/19.

18 Regulation (EC) No 1008/2008 of the European Parliament and of the Council of 24 September 2008 on common rules for the operation of air services in the Community [2008] OJ L293/3, which has superseded Regulations: (EEC) No 2407/92, (EEC) No 2408/92 and (EEC) No 2409/92.

other EU member states where the service takes place. This law also gives EU airlines freedom of combining air services and entering into code-share arrangements. Apart from the economic regulation of air services established in the 'liberalisation packages',[19] the derived law governs many other aviation relevant issues including economic regulation of airports, aviation safety and security, air navigation, aircraft manufacturing, civil liability, labour rights, environmental protection and taxes.[20]

All respective EU legal acts in these spheres will be affected by Brexit. The outcome of Brexit will, however, differ depending on the legal nature of these acts and the way they have been implemented in the UK. Legal acts of the EU consist of regulations, directives, decisions, recommendations and opinions. According to Article 288 TFEU, an EU regulation directly governs an issue. It is binding in its entirety and is directly applicable upon individuals in all member states of the EU. A directive is binding, on the member state to which it is addressed, only as to the result to be achieved. It leaves to the national authorities the choice of form and methods of regulation. A decision is binding in its entirety. It may specify to whom it is addressed and is binding only on them. Recommendations and opinions have no binding force. The important difference between directives and other EU legal acts is that the former always imply adoption of national legislation for their transposition into member states' legal orders. However, regulations, which are comprehensive by nature, may still require some implementing legislation, e.g. as regards establishment of competent executive authorities or when optional solutions are allowed at the national level.

EU law is incorporated into the British legal order[21] by virtue of the European Communities Act 1972 (ECA).[22] Section 2(1) ECA provides that EU-derived laws – which, in accordance with the Treaties, are to be given legal effect or used in the UK without further enactment (in particular EU regulations) – shall be recognised and available in British law, and be enforced, allowed and followed accordingly. EU acts which require implementation by member states are incorporated into the UK legal system by British legislation. Basically, Section 2(2) ECA empowers the government to implement them by means of secondary legislation. However, some EU laws have been implemented in the UK by separate primary legislation (Acts of Parliament) and by secondary legislation made under such primary legislation. Where UK law so provides, EU law may also be implemented by devolved legislation; however, this issue is of little significance to aviation.

---

19 See Chapter 3 of this book.
20 See Chapters 4–13 of this book. This embraces over 250 legal acts.
21 In the UK and, for certain purposes, the Channel Islands, the Isle of Man and Gibraltar.
22 European Communities Act 1972, 1972 Ch. 68.

Unless other arrangements are agreed between the UK and the EU27 on the Treaties losing their effect on the UK, all acts of derived EU law – including regulations and directives – will cease applying to the UK, its overseas and European territories and to UK-EU27 relations.[23] In such case, directly applicable acts of EU law, which make up the majority of EU aviation legislation, shall automatically have no effect in the UK and its respective territories.[24] These acts will be incorporated into the British legal system by virtue of the European Union (Withdrawal) Act.[25] Meanwhile, British legislation implementing EU laws, having been 'saved' by the European Union (Withdrawal) Act, will remain in force despite Brexit.[26] As regards EU27 member states, the EU derived law will be untouched. However, any references concerning the EU and its member states will not apply to the UK on and after Exit Day.

1.3 Domestic laws

Although a chief part of civil aviation activities in the EU is regulated directly by EU regulations, member states issue their own domestic aviation laws of varying status. Their main purpose is to regulate aviation issues lying purely within the member states' competences. However, domestic legal acts are also used to implement EU aviation laws. In the UK, the main statute in respect of civil aviation is the Civil Aviation Act 1982.[27] This Act of Parliament is supplemented by numerous items of secondary (subordinate) legislation, of which the Air Navigation Order 2016[28] plays the central role.

'Saved' by the European Union (Withdrawal) Act, British secondary legislation which implements EU-derived law will formally survive Brexit,[29] even if it will not be fully operational. Absent EU regulations, any UK laws which refer to them will have no legal effect if the corresponding norms of EU law will disappear.[30] The opposite holds true for EU directives, where comprehensive national implementing legislation is required. As explained, such UK implementing legislation will be

---

23 For the status of Gibraltar, see Chapters 1.1 and 17 of this book.
24 This is because they will no longer be acts which 'as in accordance with the Treaties are without further enactment to be given legal effect or used in the United Kingdom' referred to in Section 2(1) ECA.
25 European Union (Withdrawal) Act 2018, 2018 ch16. See also Chapter 18 of this book.
26 For the impact on British legislation, see Chapter 1.3 of this book.
27 Civil Aviation Act 1982, 1982 ch16, as amended.
28 Air Navigation Order 2016, SI 2016/765, as amended.
29 For more on the 'saving' (preservation) process, see Chapter 18 of this book.
30 Cf. L Vrbaski, 'Flying into the Unknown: The UK's Air Transport Relations with the European Union and Third Countries Following "Brexit"' (2016) 41(6) *Air & Space Law* 421, 433. However, note that regulations will be incorporated into the British legal system; see Chapter 18 of this book.

untouched by Brexit. However, it will become very problematic in practical application. First, any references to institutions of EU law included therein will become void. Second, unless the UK decides to amend them, the implementing laws will still contain references to the EU, its member states and their nationals. This will result in ridiculous asymmetry, where British law would theoretically apply to the EU27, its member states and nationals, but at least some parts of it would not apply to UK entities. These legal gaps arising from Brexit will cause a large part of UK domestic air law to be unworkable.[31] In EU27 member states domestic aviation laws including laws implementing EU law will be intact after Brexit, though any references therein concerning the EU and its member states will obviously cease to apply to the UK.

1.4 EU-third party agreements

EU law relevant to civil aviation consists not only in the Treaties and derived law, but also in a number of international agreements with third parties concerning air transport and related matters. There are several categories of international agreements concluded by the EU. Air transport is not an exclusive competence of the EU, according to the TFEU. Consequently, these agreements may be generally divided into those which are concluded with third parties by the EU itself and mixed agreements whereby the EU acts together with its member states within their shared competences. The division between EU and member state shared competences as regards third-party relations in air transport has been outlined by the CJEU in the 'Open Skies' judgement of 2002.[32] The court held that member states are not allowed to enter into international commitments containing provisions capable of affecting rules adopted by the EU or of altering their scope. Any arrangements in this respect shall be done collectively at the EU level. This, however, does not imply the automatic competence of the European Commission to negotiate aviation deals (a mandate from the Council is required). The agreements under discussion may also be divided into particular types, including agreements extending the application of EU air law, and comprehensive (vertical) and horizontal agreements. These types of agreements also present possibilities for UK-EU27 post-Brexit arrangements.[33]

---

31 This problem will require action by the British legislator. See Chapter 18 of this book.
32 Judgments of the Court of 5 November 2002 – Cases: C-466/98 *Commission v UK* [2002] ECR I-9427; C-467/98 *Commission v Denmark* [2002] ECR I-9519; C-468/98 *Commission v Sweden* [2002] ECR I-9575; C-469/98 *Commission v Finland* [2002] ECR I-9627; C-471/98 *Commission v Belgium* [2002] ECR I-9681; C-472/98 *Commission v Luxembourg* [2002] ECR I-9741; C-475/98 *Commission v Austria* [2002] ECR I-9797; C-476/98 *Commission v Germany* [2002] ECR I-9855 ('Open Skies').
33 See Chapter 17 of this book.

Unless otherwise agreed before Exit Day, all EU-third party agreements will be affected by Brexit. According to the European Council guidelines, following the withdrawal, the UK will no longer be covered by agreements concluded by the EU or by member states acting on its behalf or by the EU and its member states acting jointly, whereas the EU will continue to have its rights and obligations in relation to international agreements.[34] However, this one-size-fits-all opinion seems premature. Particularly as regards mixed agreements, its consistency with the general principles of the law of treaties may be questioned.[35] A proper evaluation of the impact of Brexit on EU-third party agreements requires careful analysis of the nature of an agreement, as well as the scope and wording of its provisions.[36]

1.4.1 Agreements extending the application of EU air law

There are agreements which, subject to additional conditions and with some modifications, extend the application of the EU air law. The first agreements of this kind were concluded by the EU with the European Free Trade Association (EFTA) member states. The primary instrument of this type was the 1992 agreement with Norway and Sweden,[37] superseded in 1994 by the agreement on the European Economic Area (EEA).[38] EU laws, including aviation laws and relevant competition laws, are

---

34 European Council, *Guidelines following the United Kingdom's notification under Article 50 TEU*, Brussels, 29 April 2017, EUCO XT 20004/17.

35 There is no reason why an EU member state would automatically cease to be bound by a mixed agreement under the *pacta sunt servanda* principle after its withdrawal from the EU. At least, the ex-member state may not invoke restrictions in the scope of the TFEU alone as a justification for its failure to perform the treaty. See Articles 27 and 46 of the Vienna Convention on the law of treaties, done at Vienna on 23 May 1969, UNTS, Vol 1155, No 18232, entered into force on 27 January 1980 ('VCTL'). But cf. the corresponding Articles of the Vienna Convention on the Law of Treaties between States and International Organizations or between International Organizations, done at Vienna, 21 March 1986, not in force. E Steinberger explains this in detail in the context of EU participation in the WTO treaty. See E Steinberger, 'The WTO Treaty as a Mixed Agreement: Problems with the EC's and the EC Member States' Membership of the WTO' (2006) 14 *European Journal of International Law* 837, 842–848.

36 This analysis should take into account the accepted methods of interpretation of treaties. See Articles 31–33 VCTL.

37 Agreement between the European Economic Community, the Kingdom of Norway and the Kingdom of Sweden on civil aviation, signed on 30 June 1992 in Brussels [1992] OJ L200/21; UNTS, Vol 1745, No 30379, not in force.

38 Agreement on the European Economic Area signed on 2 May 1992 in Porto [1994] OJ L1/3; UNTS Vol. 1793–1818, No 31121, entered into force on 1 January 1994. The agreement has expanded the application of EU aviation law to Austria, Norway, Portugal, Sweden, Iceland, Finland and Lichtenstein.

incorporated into this agreement and apply to relations between the EEA member states.[39] The EEA agreement is separate from the Treaties, though its general provisions follow their pattern. The application of derived EU legislation to the EU member states has, therefore, a double foundation stone: the TFEU and the EEA agreement (as legislation incorporated into the latter).[40]

Neither the EEA agreement nor the Treaties give any answer as to the consequences of withdrawal from the EU for the EEA agreement. The EEA agreement only provides that each contracting party may withdraw from this agreement upon 12 months' notice (Article 127). There is no reason to treat the UK's withdrawal notice to the European Council under Article 50(2) TEU as including (implicit) withdrawal from the EAA agreement.[41] There are also no circumstances that could result in the invalidity of the EEA treaty after Brexit under the law of treaties. It may be argued that, unless the UK explicitly withdraws from the EEA agreement, it will remain party to this act. In the context of Brexit, this may already raise questions concerning EU and member state shared competences, the role and scope of the UK's ratification to this agreement and the scope of provisions which remain applicable to the UK on and after Exit Day.[42] More important, however, is that after Brexit, the UK would be outside the territorial scope of the EEA agreement as set forth in its Article 126(1).[43] Also, the Preamble to the agreement and the definition of a 'Contracting Party' makes it clear that this act is an agreement between the EU, its member states and EFTA states. It does not envisage any parties of other status. These provisions imply that

39 Currently it binds Norway, Iceland and Lichtenstein, as the other countries became EU member states. Any references in the incorporated laws to the EU member states are understood as references to EFTA member states.

40 For more on the relations between EU law and the EEA agreement in air transport, see A Scheving Thorsteinsson, 'Air Transport and the Agreement on the European Economic Area' (2015) 40(4–5) *Air & Space Law* 299.

41 In particular that according to the EEA agreement, the intention to withdraw from this agreement must be notified to the contracting states of the EEA agreement.

42 The EEA agreement is a mixed agreement. Article 2(b) specifies that the term 'Contracting Parties' means, concerning the Community (now the EU) and the EC member states (now EU member states), the Community and the EC member states, or the Community, or the EC member states. The meaning to be attributed to this expression in each case is to be deduced from the relevant provisions of this Agreement and from the respective competences of the Community and the EC member states as they follow from the Treaty establishing the European Economic Community (now the TFEU).

43 The agreement shall apply to the territories to which the Treaty establishing the European Economic Community (now the TFEU) is applied and under the conditions laid down in that Treaty, and to the territories of Iceland, the Principality of Liechtenstein and the Kingdom of Norway.

after Brexit, the EEA agreement will cease to apply to the UK.[44] The UK will stop being bound by any legislation incorporated into the EEA agreement, and its relations with the mentioned EFTA sates will share the fate of UK-EU27 relations after Brexit.[45]

Switzerland – a member of EFTA which, however, did not ratify the EEA agreement – entered into separate sectoral liberalisation agreements with the EU, including one whereby the EU aviation laws incorporated into this agreement apply to Switzerland.[46] This agreement also exchanges traffic rights between Swiss and EU air carriers and introduces fair competition provisions, which are modelled on the TFEU. The provisions on traffic rights supersede the relevant provisions of existing bilateral arrangements between Switzerland and the EU member states, save for arrangements which are not covered under the EU-Swiss agreement (Article 16).[47] The latter agreement was concluded between Switzerland and the EU. By virtue of EU competences, it applies, for the EU's part, to the territories in which the TFEU is applied. Consequently, it will stop applying to the UK and UK-Swiss relations after Brexit.

One more agreement of a similar nature is the agreement on the establishment of a European Common Aviation Area (ECAA).[48] This one was concluded collectively by the EU and its members states with neighbouring Balkan states, Iceland and Norway. The ECAA is based on free market access, freedom of establishment, equal conditions of competition and common rules in the areas of safety, security, air traffic management labour protection and the environment. The agreement includes some specific provisions in these respects and extends (with some transition periods) the

---

44 Cf. L Bartels, 'The UK's status in the WTO after Brexit' (article, 23 September 2016) <www.peacepalacelibrary.nl/ebooks/files/407396411.pdf> accessed 15 June 2018. This author presents a similar reasoning in the context of GATS commitment schedules and justifies it by an analogy to the 'moving frontiers' principle.

45 For more on the impact of Brexit on the EEA agreement see C Hillion, 'Brexit means Br(EEA)xit: The UK withdrawal from the EU and its implications for the EEA' (2018) 55(1) *Common Market Law Review* 135.

46 Agreement between the European Community and the Swiss Confederation on Air Transport, signed on 21 June 1999 in Luxembourg [2002] OJ L114/73; UNTS, Vol 2227, No 39587, entered into force on 1 June 2002.

47 The EU-Swiss agreement does not cover Fifth and Seventh Freedoms rights and cabotage including points in the territories of third parties (Article 15[1] and [3] *a contrario*).

48 Multilateral Agreement between the European Community and its member states, the Republic of Albania, Bosnia and Herzegovina, the Republic of Bulgaria, the Republic of Croatia, the former Yugoslav Republic of Macedonia, the Republic of Iceland, the Republic of Montenegro, the Kingdom of Norway, Romania, the Republic of Serbia and the United Nations Interim Administration Mission in Kosovo on the establishment of a European Common Aviation Area, signed on 5 July 2006 in Luxembourg [2006] OJ L285/3, entered into force on 1 December 2017. Note that Bulgaria, Romania and Croatia have become EU member states.

application of relevant aviation *acquis communautaire* that is incorporated into the ECAA agreement. The agreement prevails over the relevant provisions of earlier bilateral air services agreements between the EU member states, Iceland and Norway on the one hand and the Balkan partners on the other hand, as well as between the Balkan partners themselves. It does not govern relations between the EEA members.

The ECAA agreement is silent about the consequences of withdrawal from the EU for this agreement. Importantly, this is a mixed agreement, which has been entered into not only by the EU but also by the UK itself. Upon the conclusion of the agreement, the UK and the EU have acted within the scope of their shared competences and the definition of 'Contracting Party' in the agreement refers to respective competences of the EU and its member states. Therefore, any provisions of the ECAA agreement that were within the EU's external competences shall automatically not apply to the UK after Brexit. This will include the main provisions of this agreement, especially those concerning application of EU derived law. Less clear is the post-Brexit status of the parts resting within UK competence, as is the scope of such parts.

On the one hand, the agreement generally refers to 'Contracting Parties' which, with regard to the EU (Community) and its member states, are the EU and the EU member states, or the EU, or the EU member states. It is specified that the meaning to be attributed to this expression in each case is to be deduced from the relevant provisions of the agreement and from the respective competences of the EU and its member states as they follow from the TFEU (Article 2[1][d]). This would theoretically allow the clauses that are within UK competence to survive Brexit. There is also no limitation of the territorial scope of the ECAA agreement on the part of the EU member states to the territories in which the TFEU is applied (a clause common in other agreements).

On the other hand, there are some general provisions in the ECAA agreement which refer directly to EU member states and would become inapplicable to the UK post-Brexit (e.g. Article 18[6], Article 20[1]), further contributing to the unworkability of the whole act. Importantly, the ECAA agreement does not provide for any special solutions concerning severability. In addition, the Preamble and Article 1 to the agreement explicitly declare that its aim is to create an area based on free market access, freedom of establishment, equal conditions of competition and common rules including in the areas of safety, security, air traffic management, labour protection and the environment. This suggests that no part of this agreement is separable from the economic provisions which are within EU competence. Therefore, it seems that the ECAA agreement will cease applying to the UK in its entirety after Brexit.

1.4.2 Vertical agreements

Historically, aviation relations between the UK and third countries were based on bilateral air services agreements, many of which are still in force.

However, more recently, some air services agreements have been developed on an EU basis. The agreements which are concluded with third parties by both the EU and its member states (mixed agreements) define traffic rights, operational rights and ancillary rights normally included in bilateral air services agreements. They also cover numerous other regulatory issues, including passenger rights, the environment, competition, safety regulation and security. Importantly, any rights arising from these agreements are attributed to all EU air carriers.

The first and economically most significant of the EU vertical agreements is the 2007 agreement between the EU and its member states and the US[49] amended by a protocol of 2010.[50] This agreement establishes a liberal regime based on the First–Fifth Freedoms and limited Seventh Freedom of the Air, free capacity, frequency and price determination open to all US and EU air carriers, extending also to Iceland and Norway.[51] During the period of provisional application, this agreement suspends[52] bilateral agreements between the US and EU member states (except to the extent related to those EU member state overseas territories in which the TFEU does not apply). This effect concerns also the restrictive UK-US Bermuda II Agreement of 1977.[53]

The parties to the 2007 agreement are the US and the EU, along with its member states. The recitals to this agreement clearly state that the UK enters the agreement being a party to the TFEU and being a member state of the EU.[54] Further, for the EU's part, all references in the agreement are to

---

49 Air Transport Agreement between the European Community and its Member States, of the one part, and the United States of America, of the other part, done at Brussels on 25 April 2007 and at Washington on 30 April 2007 [2007] OJ L134/4, provisionally applied as from 30 March 2008.

50 Protocol to amend the Air Transport Agreement between the United States of America and the European Community and its Member States, signed on 25 and 30 April 2007, signed on 24 June 2010 in Luxembourg OJ [2010] L223/3, provisionally applied as from the date of signature.

51 Based on the Air Transport Agreement between the United States of America, of the first part; the European Union and its Member States, of the second part; Iceland, of the third part; and the Kingdom of Norway, of the fourth part, signed on 16 June 2011 in Luxembourg and on 21 June 2011 in Oslo [2011] OJ L283/3, applied provisionally as from the date of signature.

52 Upon the entry into force, the agreement shall supersede the bilateral agreements (Article 22).

53 Agreement between the Government of the United States of America and the Government of the United Kingdom of Great Britain and Northern Ireland concerning Air Services (with Annexes and Exchange of letters), signed in Bermuda on 23 July 1977, UKTS 76 (1977) Cm. 7016; UNTS, Vol. 1079, No 16509, entered into force as from the date of signature.

54 As to the definition of a party to the agreement established in Article 1(6), the EU delegation has explained in the Memorandum of Consultations to the agreement that nothing in the agreement affects the distribution of competencies between the EU and its member states resulting from the TFEU.

the EU and its member states, to community airlines and to the territory in which the TFEU is applied. Therefore, even though the agreement has also been entered into by the member states within their shared competences, it will undoubtedly cease to apply in its entirety to the UK on Exit Day (currently, it applies on a provisional basis). Brexit will have a comparable legal effect on the EU-Canada air transport agreement, which is of similar scope and nature and which is also applied provisionally.[55]

The EU and its member states have also concluded vertical air transport agreements with Morocco,[56] Jordan[57] and Israel[58] (Euro-Mediterranean agreements) and with Georgia[59] and Moldova[60] (Common Aviation Area [CAA] agreements). These agreements are based on liberal market access principles. They consist of rules concerning aviation safety, the environment, economic regulation, passenger rights, consumer protection, air traffic management, competition issues and social aspects, and partly incorporate EU law in this respect. Save for rights which are not covered under these agreements, they supersede or prevail over the relevant provisions of existing bilateral agreements between the EU member states and third parties. The agreements have been concluded by the EU and its member states within their shared competences which is reflected in the definitions of the contracting parties. However, provisions of these agreements refer to community operating licenses, to ownership and control vested in EU member state nationals and to the territory in which the TFEU is applied. The Euro-Mediterranean agreements are also strictly related to special Association

---

55 Agreement on Air Transport between the European Community and its Member States, of the one part, and Canada, of the other part, done at Brussels on 17 September 2009 [2010] OJ L207/32, applied provisionally to the UK as of 28 April 2011.

56 Euro-Mediterranean aviation agreement between the European Community and its Member States, of the one part, and the Kingdom of Morocco, of the other part, signed on 12 December 2006 in Brussels [2012] OJ L386/57, entered into force on 19 March 2018.

57 Euro-Mediterranean Aviation Agreement between the European Union and its Member States, of the one part, and the Hashemite Kingdom of Jordan, of the other part, signed on 15 December 2010 in Brussels [2012] OJ L334/3, applied provisionally to the UK as of 28 April 2011.

58 Euro-Mediterranean Aviation Agreement between the European Union and its Member States, of the one part, and the government of the State of Israel, of the other part, signed on 10 June 2013 in Luxembourg [2013] OJ L208/3, applied provisionally as of the date of signature.

59 Common Aviation Area Agreement between the European Union and its Member States, of the one part, and Georgia, of the other part, signed on 2 December 2010 in Brussels [2012] OJ L321/3, applied provisionally.

60 Common Aviation Area Agreement between the European Union and its Member States and the Republic of Moldova, signed on 26 June 2012 in Brussels [2012] OJ L292/3, applied provisionally as of the date of signature.

Agreements between the Mediterranean partners and the EU. This makes all parts of these agreements inseparable from EU membership and inapplicable to the UK, post-Brexit.

After its withdrawal from the EU, the UK will not benefit from any further vertical agreements. The EU plans to enter into comprehensive air services agreements with neighbouring countries (Ukraine, Turkey, Tunisia, Azerbaijan, Lebanon, Algeria, Armenia, Egypt, Libya and Syria) and key partners (Australia, New Zealand, Brazil). The European Commission also wishes to negotiate agreements with Russia, China, India, Japan, the Gulf states and the Association of Southeast Asian Nations (ASEAN).[61] Some of these agreements are already under negotiations.

1.4.3 Horizontal agreements

Where vertical agreements do not exist, external relations of the EU member states are ruled by bilateral air services agreements concluded by the member states and third parties. These agreements usually require that substantial ownership and effective control of the parties' airlines is vested in the parties and/or in their nationals. However, such requirement has been abandoned in relations between EU member states. An airline established in an EU member state may be substantially owned or effectively controlled by any EU member states and/or their nationals, which is in conflict with the previously mentioned traditional requirement included in many bilateral agreements. Against this background, the CJEU ruled in the 2002 'Open Skies' cases that national ownership and control clauses contained within member states' air services agreements constitute an unlawful discrimination excluding air carriers of other member states from the benefit of national treatment in the host member state.

Hence, member states' air services agreements had to be brought into compliance with EU law by means of national[62] or EU action. The latter option means conclusion of special agreements with third states by the EU subject to the procedure set forth in Article 218 TFEU. The main goal of these agreements, also known as horizontal agreements, is to substitute the standard EU airline ownership and control clauses[63] for traditional national

---

61 See Commission, 'The EU's External Aviation Policy – Addressing Future Challenges' (Communication) COM/2012/0556 final.

62 See Chapter 1.5 of this book.

63 Under the latest standard clause, the air carrier designated by an EU member state should be authorised, provided that: 1) the air carrier is established under the TFEU in the territory of the designating member state and has a valid operating license in accordance with EU law; 2) effective regulatory control of the air carrier is exercised and maintained by the member state responsible for issuing its Air Operators Certificate and the relevant aeronautical

ownership and control provisions in bilateral agreements between the member states and third parties. Additionally, horizontal agreements involve provisions on safety, taxation and pricing, which are also aimed at modifying member state bilateral agreements. Currently horizontal agreements have been concluded with 41 countries and one regional organisation with eight member states. These horizontal agreements have amended 670 bilateral agreements between those countries and EU member states.[64] After Brexit, the UK will no longer be an EU member state referred to in these agreements, which will have important consequences for the UK and EU27 member states' bilateral agreements.[65]

1.4.4 Safety and security agreements

Brexit will have impact on a number of agreements concerning aviation safety and security. First, the EU has concluded a series of aviation safety agreements with nations representing key aircraft manufacturers: the US,[66] Canada[67] and Brazil.[68] These agreements provide for reciprocal acceptance of approvals concerning airworthiness, manufacturing and maintenance facilities, and environmental requirements. They also concern other forms of regulatory cooperation between the EU and its member states and third-party aviation authorities. Second, the EU has entered several agreements for the recognition of security screening rules at airports.[69] These agreements recognise that the security standards applied in third countries

---

authority is clearly identified in the designation; and 3) the air carrier is owned, directly or through majority ownership, and is effectively controlled by member states and/or nationals of member states and/or by EFTA states (Iceland, Liechtenstein, Norway, Switzerland) and/or nationals of these states. The criteria for withholding air carrier designation are analogous. In exercising its withholding rights, the foreign partner shall not discriminate between community air carriers on the grounds of nationality.

64 'Air: External Aviation Policy – Horizontal Agreements' (*Europa*, undated) <https://ec.europa.eu/transport/modes/air/international_aviation/external_aviation_policy/horizontal_agreements_en> accessed 15 June 2018.

65 See Chapter 1.5 of this book.

66 Agreement between the United States of America and the European Community on cooperation in the regulation of civil aviation safety, signed in Brussels on 30 June 2008 [2011] OJ L291/3, entered into force on 1 May 2011.

67 Agreement on civil aviation safety between the European Community and Canada, signed in Prague on 6 May 2009 [2009] OJ L153/11, entered into force on 26 July 2011.

68 Agreement between the European Union and the Government of the Federative Republic of Brazil on civil aviation safety, signed in Brasília on 14 July 2010 [2011] OJ L273/3, entered into force on 27 August 2013.

69 Such agreements have been concluded with: the US, Canada, Montenegro, Faroe Islands (in regard to Vagar airport), Greenland (in regard to Kangerlussuaq airport), Guernsey, Jersey, the Isle of Man and Singapore.

are equivalent to EU standards and allow for one-stop security for flights between those countries and EU member states. Third, the EU entered into a cooperation agreement whereby the International Civil Aviation Organisation (ICAO) has assigned to the European Commission the inspections of EU member states' national authorities. These inspections are aimed to verify compliance with aviation security standards included in Annex 17 to the Chicago Convention.[70] Finally, there are international instruments which refer to passenger data (Passenger Name Record, or PNR) that are collected by EU member states for security reasons. PNR data are exchanged with other countries based on special agreements. There are currently three such agreements: with the US,[71] Canada[72] and Australia.[73] The PNR agreements envisage that carriers operating from the EU to the other party of the agreement process PNR data as required by the competent authority of this party. The previously mentioned safety and security agreements have been concluded by the EU within the scope of its competences and are binding upon EU member states. After the UK's withdrawal from the EU, they will cease applying in their entirety to Britain and to operations between the UK and third states. Consequently, the UK may need to arrange for new agreements in this respect or renegotiate existing bilateral agreements with some of its overseas partners.[74]

1.5 EU member states' bilateral agreements

There are several groups of bilateral air services agreements concluded by the EU member states with third parties that will be affected by Brexit. As already mentioned, in the 2002 'Open Skies' judgements, the CJEU

---

70 Memorandum of Cooperation between the International Civil Aviation Organisation and the European Community regarding security audits/inspections and related matters, signed at Montreal on 17 September 2008 [2009] OJ L36/19, applied provisionally as of the date of signature.

71 Agreement between the United States of America and the European Union on the use and Transfer of Passenger Name Records to the United States Department of Homeland Security, signed in Brussels on 14 December 2011 [2012] OJ L215/5; UNTS, No 52729, entered into force on 1 July 2012.

72 Agreement between the European Community and the Government of Canada on the processing of Advance Passenger Information and Passenger Name Record data signed in Luxembourg on 3 October 2005 [2006] OJ L82/15; UNTS, Vol. 2467, No 44329, entered into force on 22 March 2006.

73 Agreement between the European Union and Australia on the processing and transfer of Passenger Name Record (PNR) data by air carriers to the Australian Customs and Border Protection Service, signed in Brussels on 29 September 2011 [2012] OJ L186/4, entered into force on 1 June 2012.

74 See also Chapters 6–7 of this book.

disqualified national ownership and control clauses in member states' air services agreements. Consequently, many of the member states' bilateral agreements have been modified by means of horizontal agreements which replaced the national ownership and control clauses with EU standard clauses.[75] The impact of Brexit on the horizontally amended bilateral agreements will depend on the configuration of parties to these agreements. In the EU27-third party forum, the amended agreements will still apply; however, after Brexit, the UK will not be considered an EU member state referred to in horizontal agreements and thus will be deprived of the benefits arising from the EU standard clauses. The impact of Brexit is much less clear as regards the UK-third party bilateral agreements which have been modified by horizontal agreements. Notably, Brexit itself does not change the fact that horizontal agreements remain fully binding for the UK's aviation partners (third states).

On the one hand, it could be argued that on and after Exit Day, all references to EU member states in horizontal agreements, including those to bilateral agreements between the third party and an EU member state, will simply not concern the UK. This view could be supported by the aim of horizontal agreements as declared in their preambles, which is bringing EU member states' air services agreements into conformity with EU law. Such an interpretation would mean that after Brexit, horizontal agreements will cease to apply to the UK's bilateral agreements in general and that the latter shall regain their original wording.

On the other hand, the specific language of the horizontal agreements suggests that the role of these agreements is not to establish a new regime between EU member states and third states that would modify the application of parallel bilateral regimes (and that would by definition not apply to ex-member states), but rather to amend the wording of existing EU member states' bilateral agreements. Remarkably, horizontal agreements speak of superseding and complementing the provisions of member states' air services agreements, not of suspending them or prevailing over them. Hence, once the horizontal change to bilateral agreements has taken effect,[76] it may only be reversed by subsequent amendment to these agreements. Until that happens, the UK will not be considered an EU member state referred to in its own bilateral agreements and will be deprived of rights arising from these agreements, unlike the EU27 member states that would still be covered. This situation would be unacceptable for the UK, and Britain would need to renegotiate its horizontally amended bilateral agreements.

---

75 See Chapter 1.4.3 of this book
76 That is, upon the entry into force of the horizontal agreement (see Article 9 of the model horizontal agreement).

Of the two presented reasonings concerning the relation between the UK's bilateral agreements and its horizontal agreements, it would be safer to accept the second one.[77] Although highly inconvenient for the UK, this interpretation is strongly grounded on the literal reading of horizontal agreements. In this context, the UK should take into account that it will also be for the EU, its 27 member states and almost 50 third states to interpret and apply horizontal agreements after Brexit.

The other method of bringing bilateral agreements in line with EU law are bilateral negotiations led by EU member states. EU regulation 847/2004[78] allows any member state to enter into negotiations with a third country concerning a new air services agreement or a modification of an existing air services agreement, the subject matter of which falls partly within the competence of the EU, provided that relevant standard clauses are entered into such negotiations[79] and a special notification procedure is complied with. This technique has been used by EU member states to change rules with 73 third countries representing 340 bilateral agreements,[80] including some recently negotiated UK air services agreements.[81] After the UK's exit from the EU, the community standard clauses contained in the EU27-third party bilateral agreements will still be in place and will simply not cover UK nationals and airlines. Brexit will have the same effect on the UK air services agreements. This will lead to a paradoxical situation, just as in the case of horizontally amended agreements, whereby only EU27 airlines and nationals would be encompassed by the UK-third party deals. However, the UK shall be able to renegotiate its bilateral agreements or to terminate them (also on the grounds of the *rebus sic stantibus* principle).[82]

---

77 Cf. L Vrbaski, 'Flying into the Unknown: The UK's Air Transport Relations with the European Union and Third Countries Following "Brexit"' (2016) 41(6) *Air & Space Law* 421, 426–427.

78 Regulation (EC) No 847/2004 of the European Parliament and of the Council of 29 April 2004 on the negotiation and implementation of air service agreements between member states and third countries, OJ L 157, 30.4.2004, pp. 7–17.

79 Such clauses, which are more less equivalent to provisions of horizontal agreements, have been adopted in Commission Decision 29/03/2005 on approving the standard clauses for inclusion in bilateral air service agreements between member states and third countries jointly laid down by the Commission and the member states C(2005)943.

80 Air: External Aviation Policy – Horizontal Agreements' (*Europa*, undated) <https://ec.europa.eu/transport/modes/air/international_aviation/external_aviation_policy/horizontal_agreements_en> accessed 15 June 2018.

81 See, e.g. Agreement between the Government of the United Kingdom of Great Britain and Northern Ireland and the Government of Ukraine Concerning Air Services, done in Kiev on 21 November 2011, UKTS 5 (2016), Cm. 9188.

82 However, the termination shall concern the whole agreement, because ownership and control clauses are a crucial element of air services agreements and are not separable from the rest of their provisions (See Article 44 VCLT).

The UK has also signed a number of bilateral air services agreements with EU27 member states and with third parties which currently have no effect due to subsequent EU derived law, EU-third party agreements which extend the EU aviation regime and EU-third party vertical agreements. It will be interesting to see if these bilateral agreements are fully revived in relation to the UK after the previously mentioned EU-based acts have stopped applying to Britain. *Prima facie*, it may appear that when these acts cease applying to the UK, the relations between the UK and its aviation partners should be governed by previous arrangements. However, in the context of Brexit, the actual relation between such arrangements and the EU-based instruments will depend on the status and wording of the latter.

Most of these instruments speak of superseding provisions of bilateral agreements that concern matters governed by these instruments or of superseding some restrictions arising from bilateral agreements. This will be construed as termination of the relevant provisions (restrictions) included in the bilateral agreements,[83] which implies that the arrangements between the UK and its bilateral partners will not automatically regain their previous wording after Brexit. This mechanism concerns those EU instruments and UK bilateral agreements which will be in force as of the day preceding Exit Day. Currently this would encompass regulation 1008/2008, which supersedes some restrictions in bilateral agreements between EU member states,[84]

---

83 L Vrbaski rightly claims that to supersede is to annul, make void, or repeal by taking the place of. He also points out that this interpretation is supported by the fact that e.g. the EU-US air transport agreement expressly identifies two different effects on prior agreements, i.e. suspension and supersession. See 'Flying into the Unknown', p. 435.

84 Contrary to some opinions, bilateral agreements between EU member states have not been superseded (terminated) in whole by virtue of regulation 1008/2008. Notably, this regulation speaks only twice of superseding some restrictions arising from bilateral agreements. Article 15(4) clause 2 states that '[a]ny restrictions on the freedom of Community air carriers to operate intra-Community air services arising from bilateral agreements between Member States are hereby superseded'. This shall be understood in the context of the first clause which already permits combining air services and entering into code-share arrangements in intra-Community air services. The aim of clause 2 is, thus, to supersede other possible operational restrictions concerning intra-Community services that otherwise would not be overruled by specific provisions of regulation 1008/2008; e.g. Article 15(4) clause 2 shall not cover the airline ownership and control rules incorporated in bilateral agreements, since these rules are already directly governed by Chapter II of regulation 1008/2008 which prevails over the bilateral agreements. At the same time, Article 15(4) clause 2 shall cover bilateral restrictions on capacity and frequency because regulation 1008/2008 does not include provisions in this respect (save for Public Service Obligation [PSO] rules). This logic is explicitly reflected in Article 22(2) clause 2 which supersedes 'any *remaining* restrictions on pricing, including with respect to routes to third countries, arising from bilateral agreements between Member States' (emphasis added). In particular, there is no reason to believe that bilaterally exchanged traffic rights are a restriction referred to in Article 15(4) clause 2. These provisions establish rights for air carriers, that only later may

and the EEA agreement, which extends this effect to EEA member states, as well as the EU-Swiss aviation agreement and the Euro-Mediterranean aviation agreement with Morocco, which speak of superseding all relevant provisions of bilateral agreements[85] that concern matters overlapping with these vertical agreements.

The same problems will concern the provisionally applied EU-US and EU-Canada air transport agreements and Euro-Mediterranean aviation agreements with Israel and Jordan; however, only if these agreements enter into force before Brexit. Unless that happens, the provisionally applied EU vertical agreements only suspend the application of the relevant British bilateral arrangements (not supersede their provisions),[86] which means that the application of these bilateral arrangements could be resumed in whole after Brexit.

Brexit will have similar effect with respect to the ECAA agreement and the CAA agreements with Moldova and Georgia. These three agreements speak of prevailing over (not superseding) the relevant provisions of existing bilateral agreements,[87] which indicates that these provisions have not been terminated. The ECAA and CAA agreements affect only the current application but not the contents of relevant bilateral agreements. Hence, after Brexit, the old British bilateral agreements with ECAA partners (other than EEA member states) and CAA partners will keep their original wording and will once again be fully applicable. However, in practice, the application of at least some of these revived agreements may be problematic, since they will not be adequate to support the current air traffic. The same is true of those UK-third party bilateral agreements the application of which is now suspended by EU vertical agreements and will be resumed after Brexit. This is because the revived British bilateral agreements are usually more restrictive in terms of traffic rights, capacity, tariffs and operational rights than the current EU-based regimes.[88]

Finally, the EU member states including the UK have also concluded with third parties some air services agreements that follow traditional bilateral

---

be restricted in other parts of bilateral agreements. Indeed, if the intention of regulation 1008/2008 was to supersede (not to prevail over) all relevant provisions of bilateral agreements, including the traffic rights exchange, this would be established explicitly, as in e.g. the EU-Swiss aviation agreement.

85 Between EU member states and Switzerland or Morocco, respectively.
86 This effect stems from the nature of provisional application and the good faith principle. In the EU-US and EU-Canada air transport agreements, this effect has been expressly confirmed (Articles 22 and 26, respectively).
87 See Article 28 of the ECAA agreement and Article 25 in each of the CAA agreements. Such effect is independent of the entry into force of the CAA agreements or their provisional application.
88 See also Chapter 3 of this book.

patterns and that have not been interfered with by any EU instruments (including agreements which extend the application of EU air law, vertical agreements and horizontal agreements). Brexit will be neutral for these kind of agreements. The group of Brexit-resistant bilateral provisions will also embrace those rules in air services agreements that have not been superseded by regulation 1008/2008 or by EU-third party agreements.

1.6 WTO framework

The World Trade Organization (WTO) legal framework includes a number of instruments, of which only a few are related to civil aviation. The main WTO instrument which deals with aviation issues is the General Agreement on Trade in Services (GATS),[89] which refers to trade in services. This treaty is based on the Most Favoured Nation (MFN) clause upon which the best conditions that have been conceded to one state-party must be automatically applied to all other GATS participants. GATS also provides for commitments concerning market access and national treatment (absence of discriminatory measures against foreign services or service suppliers). These commitments, which may be sectoral or horizontal, are made in special schedules and each party to GATS is required to submit a Schedule of Specific Commitments. However, according to the Annex on Air Transport Services, hard traffic rights, which are the domain of bilateral air services agreements, have been excluded from the scope of GATS. Consequently, the agreement applies only to measures concerning aircraft repair and maintenance services (except for line maintenance), selling and marketing of air transport services (excluding pricing of air transport services) and computer reservation systems (CRS) services. Thus, only these services, commonly referred to as ancillary services, are subject to the MFN clause and to specific commitments in air transport.

Both the EU and its member states are parties to GATS. However, contrary to the EU-third party aviation agreements,[90] GATS and the whole WTO agreement[91] do not include any arrangements concerning competences of the parties and the corresponding scope of exercised rights. These instruments also do not allow for any reservations or partial consent to their

---

89 General Agreement on Trade in Services – Annex 1B of the Agreement Establishing the World Trade Organization, done in Marrakesh on 15 April 1994, UNTS, Vol. 1869, No 31874, entered into force on 1 January 1995.
90 See Chapter 1.4 of this book.
91 Marrakesh Agreement establishing the World Trade Organization, done in Marrakesh on 15 April 1994, UNTS, Vol. 1867, No 31874, entered into force on 1 January 1995.

provisions.[92] On the one hand, this suggests that the UK has ratified the WTO agreement without any limitations and that Brexit will not upset the UK's rights and obligations arising from this agreement. This argument finds some confirmation in WTO jurisprudence. On the other hand, GATS embraces matters that are within EU competence. The CJEU has clarified in its opinion that cross-border supply falls within the concept of the common commercial policy which is the subject of exclusive EU competence (Article 3[1][e] TFEU), whereas other modes of supply of services referred to by GATS are shared competences. What is more, TFEU provisions on transport services are distinct from the common commercial policy and by virtue of Article 4(2)(g) belong in whole to the shared competences.[93] This could suggest that after Brexit, GATS would not bind the UK in the areas of EU competence. Both views can be justified by the general international rules concerning observance and interpretation of treaties; however, more convincing are the arguments for the full membership of the EU member states in the WTO and consequently for the full application of GATS to the UK after Brexit.[94]

However, even this concept still does not resolve the issue of specific commitments to GATS. As regards the EU and its member states, the specific commitments to GATS have been made jointly (this concerns i.a. specific commitments as to Sector 11.C – Air Transport Services) and are subject to the limitation that they apply only to the territories in which the TFEU is applied and only to the relations between the EU and its member states on the one hand, and non-EU countries on the other. It seems, therefore, that after Brexit, these commitments will become unclear, if not void, in respect of the UK and its territory, and that London will need to submit new schedules, including Sector 11.C.[95]

---

92 Consent of a state to be bound by part of a treaty is effective only if the treaty so permits or the other contracting states so agree. It may also arise from reservations to the treaty, provided that they were not prohibited (Articles 17, 19, 23 VCLT).

93 Opinion No 1/94 of the Court of 15 November 1994, *Competence of the Community to conclude international agreements concerning services and the protection of intellectual property – Article 228 (6) of the EC Treaty.*

94 See: L Bartels, 'The UK's status in the WTO after Brexit' (article, 23 September 2016) <www.peacepalacelibrary.nl/ebooks/files/407396411.pdf> accessed 15 June 2018; E Steinberger, 'The WTO Treaty as a Mixed Agreement: Problems with the EC's and the EC Member States' Membership of the WTO' (2006) 14 *European Journal of International Law* 837, 855–857.

95 See L Bartels, 'The UK's status in the WTO after Brexit' (article, 23 September 2016) <www.peacepalacelibrary.nl/ebooks/files/407396411.pdf> accessed 15 June 2018. Note that the EU may also wish to modify its schedule and withdraw commitments to reflect the UK's withdrawal from the EU, see P Delimatsis, 'The Evolution of the EU External Trade

Another WTO instrument that has been important for the aviation sector is the WTO Agreement on Subsidies and Countervailing Measures (SCM Agreement).[96] The agreement defines particular types of subsidies as prohibited or actionable, provides for consultations and dispute settlement procedures and regulates the application of countervailing measures. It is a cross-sector act which relates to trade in goods and does not apply to airlines. However, it does apply to subsidies to manufacturers of civil aircraft and has been the basis for a number of claims in this respect. Just as have other multilateral WTO treaties, the SCM agreement has been entered into by both the EU and its member states. The SCM agreement provisions concern matters that are relevant to the exercise of EU exclusive competences regarding commercial policy and competition rules (Article 3[2] TFEU). However, once again, the previously mentioned arguments concerning the nature of the WTO agreement speak for the full applicability of the SCM Agreement to the UK before and after Brexit.

Finally, there is one more part of the WTO legacy which is relevant to aviation. This is the Agreement on Trade in Civil Aircraft,[97] which has accompanied the General Agreement on Tariffs and Trade (GATT 1947)[98] since 1980. It eliminates import duties on all civil aircraft, as well as on civil aircraft engines and their parts and components, as well as on all components and sub-assemblies of civil aircraft, and flight simulators and their parts and components (however, not unfinished products or raw materials). It also embraces other provisions i.a. on government-directed procurement and establishment of trade restrictions. The Agreement on Trade in Civil Aircraft is a plurilateral agreement which has been entered into *inter alia*

Policy in Services – CETA, TTIP, and TiSA after Brexit' (2017) 20 *Journal of International Economic Law* 583, 594–595. The same may apply to third countries. However, given the modest range of aviation-related commitments, it is unlikely that these commitments would be subject to revision on the EU's part.

96 Agreement on Subsidies and Countervailing Measures, part of the Multilateral Agreements on Trade in Goods – Annex 1A of the Agreement Establishing the World Trade Organization, done in Marrakesh on 15 April 1994, UNTS, Vol 1869, No 31874, entered into force on 1 January 1995.

97 Agreement on Trade in Civil Aircraft, done in Geneva on 12 April 1979, UNTS, 1186, Vol 814, entered into force on 1 January 1980, now incorporated in the Agreement Establishing the World Trade Organization done in Marrakesh on 15 April 1994 as its Annex 4(a).

98 General Agreement on Tariffs and Trade signed in Geneva on 30 October 1947 (GATT 1947), UNTS, Vol. 55, No 814, applied as of 1 January 1948, now incorporated in the General Agreement on Tariffs and Trade of 1994 (GATT 1994) as part of the Multilateral Agreements on Trade in Goods – Annex 1A of the Agreement Establishing the World Trade Organization, done in Marrakesh on 15 April 1994, UNTS, Vol. 1867, No 31874, entered into force on 1 January 1995.

by the EU and some of its member states including the UK.[99] Most matters covered by this agreement lie within the exclusive competences of the EU (customs, trade policy). Nevertheless, given the nature of WTO instruments as discussed previously, this agreement shall also remain applicable to the UK on and after Exit Day. Brexit will, however, change the performance of the agreement. This is because the EU, acting within its exclusive competence, has entered into a bilateral agreement with the US concerning the application of the agreement in question to large civil aircraft.[100] The latter instrument will be inapplicable to the UK after Brexit.

The EU and its member states have also entered into numerous free trade agreements with third parties establishing free trade areas envisaged in Article XXIV GATT 1994 and Article V GATS. As regards aviation, the rights concerning cross-border supply, investment and establishment exchanged in these agreements may transcend the catalogue incorporated in the GATS Annex on Air Transport Services and embrace also ground-handling services, rental service of aircraft with crew and airport management services (though this may be subject to reservations).[101] For the EU's part, these free trade agreements apply to the territories in which the TFEU and TEU are applied, which means that they shall cease to apply to the UK post-Brexit irrespective of the UK's ratification. The UK will also be excluded from the future free trade agreements which are currently being negotiated by the EU.

1.7 Cape Town Convention

The simultaneous adoption of the Cape Town Convention (CTC) on international interests in mobile equipment[102] and its aircraft protocol[103] by the

---

99 The others being Austria, Belgium, Bulgaria, Denmark, Estonia, France, Germany, Greece, Ireland, Italy, Latvia, Lithuania, Luxembourg, Malta, the Netherlands, Portugal, Romania, Spain and Sweden.
100 Agreement between the European Economic Community and the Government of the United States of America concerning the application of the GATT Agreement on Trade in Civil Aircraft on trade in large civil aircraft, signed at Brussels and Washington on 17 July 1992 [1992] OJ L301/32, entered into force as from the date of signature.
101 See, e.g. Comprehensive Economic and Trade Agreement (CETA) between Canada, of the one part, and the European Union and its Member States, of the other part, done in Brussels on 30 October 2016, OJ L 11, 14.1.2017, pp. 23–1079, applied provisionally as from 21 September 2017.
102 Convention on International Interests in Mobile Equipment, signed at Cape Town on 16 November 2001, ICAO Doc 9793; UNTS, Vol. 2307, No 41143, entered into force on 1 March 2006.
103 Protocol to the Convention on international interests in mobile equipment on matters specific to aircraft equipment, signed at Cape Town on 16 November 2001, ICAO Doc 9794; UNTS, Vol 2367, No 41143, entered into force on 1 March 2006.

UK and the EU will have similar consequences to those arising from the parallel participation of the UK and the EU in GATS.[104] Unlike many other mixed EU-third party agreements, the Cape Town acts do not refer, for the EU's part, to the territories where the TFEU is applied, or to EU member states as such. Hence, the wording of these acts itself does not preclude their application to the UK on the day of and after the UK's exit. It also seems that the UK's ratification of the CTC and its aircraft protocol will be fully valid after Brexit despite the separate EU accession within its competences as a Regional Economic Integration Organisation (REIO).[105] None of the CTC or protocol provisions limit the rights and obligations of REIO member states under these acts due to the REIO's parallel accession to these acts. On the contrary, it is the REIO's rights that are limited.[106] Furthermore, the CTC and the protocol do not allow state parties to accept only parts of these acts nor to express reservations thereto. This *per se* precludes the possibility that the UK could ratify these acts only as regards matters encompassed by its own competences as an EU member state. The division of competences between REIOs and their member states is relevant only as regards the performance of the CTC and the protocol by their parties. In particular, it decides on the scope of possible declarations to be lodged under the CTC and the protocol.[107] Accordingly, the UK and the EU have made declarations as to some matters lying within their competences. Therefore, when, after leaving the EU, the UK obtains competences concerning all issues previously in the possession of the EU, Britain should consider lodging its own declaration in this respect. At the same time, the declarations already made by the UK will be intact after Brexit.

---

104 See Chapter 1.6 of this book.
105 The EU has acceded to the CTC and the protocol according to Article 48 CTC and Article XXVII of the protocol which provide that a REIO which is constituted by sovereign states and has competence over certain matters governed by the CTC and the protocol may sign, accept, approve or accede to the CTC (and the protocol), and that the REIO shall, at the time of signature, acceptance, approval or accession, make a declaration to the Depositary specifying the matters governed by the CTC and the protocol in respect of which competence has been transferred to that REIO by its member states. The declarations lodged by the EU under the CTC and the protocol at the time of the deposit of its instruments of accession refer to the transfer of competences to the EU by its member states and specify the scope of transferred competences.
106 The REIO shall have the rights and obligations of a contracting state, to the extent that the organisation has competence over matters governed by the CTC and the protocol.
107 For a digest of arguments concerning the UK's post-Brexit status as a party to the CTC and the protocol, see: K Gray, 'CTC in Europe assessment of ratifications to date and implications of Brexit on the ratification by the UK' (2016) 5(1) *Cape Town Convention Journal* 1, 18–21.

2 Brexit-resistant legal acts

Some international aviation treaties and agreements to which the UK is a party will not be disturbed by Brexit. These acts usually concern those parts of air law that are not covered by EU transport policy and regulation. However, some of these instruments, although formally untouched by Brexit, may enjoy some sort of relationship with EU law, and this relationship will change after Brexit. Finally, it is worth mentioning that the unaffected international agreements will constitute the foundations of post-Brexit aviation regulation applicable to the UK and its relations with aviation partners.

2.1 ICAO framework

The ICAO framework, which constitutes the Chicago Convention with Annexes and two treaties on air freedoms, will be entirely intact after Brexit. The Chicago Convention was adopted nearly 75 years ago, and it has become the constitution of international civil aviation. Currently, its parties include the UK, all EU27, EFTA and ECAA states (except Kosovo) and the parties to the EU vertical agreements. Even after Brexit, all UK aviation relations with these countries will continue to be based on the principles of this convention.

The convention, together with its Annexes, concerns mainly technical aspects of air navigation, which will be referred to later in this book. However, a few of its articles deal with commercial aspects of air transport. Under Article 6 of the convention, any scheduled air service[1] requires a

---

1 ICAO Council Resolution A2–18 of 1952 defines 'scheduled international air service' as a service which: 1) passes through the airspace over the territory of more than one state, 2) is performed by aircraft for the transportation of passengers, mail or cargo for remuneration in such a manner that each flight is open to use by members of the public, and 3) is operated so as to serve traffic between the same two or more points, either according to a published timetable or with flights so regular or frequent that they constitute a recognisable systematic series.

special permission or authorisation from the country to which the service is supplied. This very requirement leads to the conclusion of bilateral air services agreements which specify the conditions for these permissions or authorisations. Unlike scheduled air services, non-scheduled operations are allowed by virtue of Article 5 of the convention, which provides that a civil aircraft registered in a contracting state has the authority, unless it is engaged in scheduled international air service, to fly into other contracting states or make non-stop transit across their territories or make stops for non-traffic purposes there, without a need to obtain a prior permission from the states concerned. Notably, this privilege is attached to the aircraft (not airline). However, as regards commercial flights, this right may be subject to additional conditions or limitations imposed by the contracting states. Notwithstanding, it is established in Article 7 of the convention that each contracting state has the right to refuse cabotage, i.e. the permission to the aircraft of other contracting states to take on in its territory passengers, mail and cargo carried for remuneration or hire and destined for another point within its territory. While Article 5 of the Chicago Convention is less important in the context of Brexit, Article 6 and possibly Article 7 will be the legal base for any post-Brexit arrangements that need to be made in UK-EU27 and UK-third party relations, that is in relations where air services will lose their current legal framework arising from EU law and EU-based international agreements.

There have been many attempts to overcome the restrictions of scheduled international air services arising from Article 6. However, no general multilateral agreement on economic issues in civil aviation has ever been reached. Nonetheless, two other instruments were adopted together with the Chicago Convention. First is the International Air Services Transit Agreement,[2] which defines the first two technical Freedoms of the Air. Second is the International Air Transport Agreement,[3] which organises five Freedoms of the Air in respect of scheduled international air services.[4] The International Air Services Transit Agreement has been ratified by 131

---

2 International Air Services Transit Agreement, signed at Chicago on 7 December 1944, ICAO Doc 9587; UNTS, Vol 84, No 252, entered into force on 30 January 1945.

3 International Air Transport Agreement, signed at Chicago on 7 December 1944, ICAO Doc 9587; UNTS, Vol 17, No 502, entered into force on 8 February 1945.

4 The five Freedoms of the Air defined in this Agreement include: 1) the privilege to fly across contracting state's territory without landing; 2) the privilege to land for non-traffic purposes; 3) the privilege, in respect of scheduled international air services, to put down passengers, mail and cargo taken on in the territory of the state whose nationality the aircraft possesses; 4) the privilege, in respect of scheduled international air services, to take on passengers, mail and cargo destined for the territory of the state whose nationality the aircraft possesses; and 5) the privilege, in respect of scheduled international air services, to take on passengers, mail and cargo destined for the territory of any other contracting state and the privilege to

parties including the UK, EU27 (except Lithuania and Romania), EFTA (except Liechtenstein) and ECAA states (except Kosovo), as well as by the parties to EU vertical agreements (except Canada). The International Air Transport Agreement has been ratified by only 11 states, and the UK is not a party to this agreement.

2.2 ECAC framework

The UK, which is a member of the European Civil Aviation Conference (ECAC), has joined several conventions adopted under the auspices of this organisation. One of them, the Multilateral Agreement on Commercial Rights of Non-Scheduled Air Services,[5] is still binding between the UK and many of its European aviation partners,[6] although EU regulation 1008/2008 and EU-third party agreements currently prevail over this multilateral instrument.[7] What is more, regulation 1008/2008 now equates the scheduled and non-scheduled air services. However, after the UK's departure from the EU, the application of this agreement could be restored. This could work to secure some non-scheduled flights on European routes that

---

put down passengers, mail and cargo coming from any such territory. Freedoms 1 and 2 are called technical freedoms or transit rights, whereas the Third–Fifth Freedoms constitute commercial freedoms or traffic rights. Other commercial freedoms are also distinguished. These are: 6) the privilege, in respect of scheduled international air services, of transporting, via the home state of the carrier, traffic moving between two other states; 7) the privilege, in respect of scheduled international air services, of transporting traffic between the territory of the granting state and any third state with no requirement to include on such operation any point in the territory of the recipient state, i.e. the service need not connect to or be an extension of any service to or from the home state of the carrier; 8) the right or privilege, in respect of scheduled international air services, of transporting cabotage traffic between two points in the territory of the granting state on a service which originates or terminates in the home country of the foreign carrier or (in connection with the so-called Seventh Freedom of the Air) outside the territory of the granting state (also known as 'consecutive cabotage'); and 9) the right or privilege of transporting cabotage traffic of the granting state on a service performed entirely within the territory of the granting state (also known as 'stand-alone' cabotage). See *Manual on the Regulation of International Air Transport*, ICAO Doc 9626.

5 Multilateral Agreement on Commercial Rights of Non-Scheduled Air Services in Europe, done in Paris on 30 April 1956, ICAO Doc 7695; UNTS, Vol 310, No 4494, entered into force on 21 August 1957.

6 Austria, Belgium, Croatia, Denmark, Estonia, Finland, France, Germany, Hungary, Iceland, Ireland, Italy, Luxembourg, Moldova, the Netherlands, Norway, Portugal, San Marino, Spain, Sweden, Switzerland and Turkey.

7 See Article 30(3)–(4) VCLT. Importantly, provisions of the ECAC multilateral agreement have not been superseded by regulation 1008/2008 or by EU-third party agreements. This is because these instruments speak of superseding only selected restrictions and only as regards earlier bilateral agreements.

would be legally orphaned by Brexit. Nonetheless, it would not apply to scheduled air services.

Alongside the mentioned ECAC multilateral agreement on traffic rights, ECAC has sponsored an agreement on air tariffs. The 1967 agreement on the procedure for the establishment of tariffs for scheduled air services[8] links the UK with some EU/EEA member states.[9] Within this forum, regulation 1008/2008 currently prevails over the ECAC agreement. It is, however, unlikely that this tariff agreement could be revived in the UK-EU27 relations post-Brexit. It allows for price consultations between airlines, which infringes on EU competition law. Therefore, it will not be possible for the EU27 member states to base their future relations with the UK on such arrangements.

The ECAC members have also entered into an agreement on certificates of airworthiness of imported aircraft.[10] The agreement concerns validation of certificates of airworthiness for aircraft imported from one state to another. This mechanism may have some use between the UK and some of its European aviation partners[11] if the EU airworthiness rules will not apply to the UK post-Brexit.[12]

2.3 EUROCONTROL framework

The UK is a party to the EUROCONTROL Convention[13] and is one of the original members of EUROCONTROL, an institution that deals with air traffic management across Europe. Currently, EUROCONTROL has 41 member states, including all EU member states. The EUROCONTROL Convention has been amended several times[14] and supplemented with a

---

8 International Agreement on the Procedure for the Establishment of Tariffs for Scheduled Air Services, done in Paris on 10 July 1967, ICAO Doc 8681; UNTS, Vol 696, No 9971, entered into force on 30 May 1968.
9 Note that the UK is not party to the 1987 ECAC tariff agreement.
10 Multilateral Agreement relating to Certificates of Airworthiness for Imported Aircraft, done in Paris on 22 April 1960, ICAO Doc 8056; UNTS, Vol 418, No 6023, entered into force on 24 August 1961.
11 Austria, Denmark, France, Greece, Ireland, Italy, Luxembourg, the Netherlands, Norway, Portugal, Spain, Sweden and Switzerland.
12 See also Chapter 6 of this book.
13 EUROCONTROL International Convention relating to co-operation for the safety of air navigation, signed in Brussels on 13 December 1960, UNTS, Vol 523, No 7557, entered into force on 1 March 1963.
14 Additional Protocol to the EUROCONTROL International Convention relating to co-operation for the safety of air navigation, done in Brussels on 6 July 1970, UNTS, Vol 834, No 7557, entered into force on 1 August 1972; Protocol for the amendment of the Additional Protocol of 6 July 1970 to the Convention of 13 December 1960, done on

separate agreement on route charges.[15] EUROCONTROL entered into cooperation agreements with the European Commission and NATO in 2003, and since 2010 it has also been mandated with some tasks by the EU. Some aspects of air traffic management are within the EU shared competences. Therefore, the EU has decided to join EUROCONTROL with the aim of exercising these competences at the forum of this organisation.[16] It has also concluded a high-level agreement for enhanced cooperation with EUROCONTROL in 2012.[17]

Brexit shall have no impact on the EUROCONTROL Convention itself, or on its application to the UK. Although the air traffic management matters are within the EU's competences, the UK has entered the convention and the amending protocols acting as a sovereign state, without any limitations. Notably, this occurred prior to the EU's decision on accession to EURO-CONTROL. What is more, the EU is yet not a party to the EUROCON-TROL Convention, and only some parts of the protocol on accession apply provisionally. Accession is subject not only to the ratification of the relevant protocol, but also to the entry into force of the consolidating protocol of 1997, that enables this accession. Therefore, there is no doubt that the UK's ratifications of the EUROCONTROL Convention and protocols will remain valid after its exit from the EU. The same applies to the agreement on route charges. The EUROCONTROL cooperation agreements with the European Commission and NATO will also be intact.

2.4 Civil liability conventions

Civil liability issues in aviation were already unified at the international level already in the 1929 Warsaw Convention,[18] which has been amended

---

21 November 1978 in Brussels, UNTS, Vol 1437, No 7557, entered into force on 1 January 1981; Protocol amending the EUROCONTROL International Convention relating to co-operation for the safety of air navigation of 13 December 1960, done in Brussels on 12 February 1981, UNTS, Vol 1430, No 7557, entered into force on 1 January 1986. On 27 June 1997, a protocol was signed in Brussels to consolidate the EUROCONTROL Convention, but it is yet not in force.

15 Multilateral Agreement relating to Route Charges done in Brussels on 12 February 1981, UNTS, Vol 1430, No 24254, entered into force on 1 January 1986.

16 Protocol on the accession of the European Community to the EUROCONTROL International Convention relating to Cooperation for the Safety of Air Navigation of 13 December 1960, as variously amended and as consolidated by the Protocol of 27 June 1997, done in Brussels on 8 October 2002 [2004] OJ L304/210, not in force.

17 Agreement between the European Union and the European Organisation for the Safety of Air Navigation providing a general framework for enhanced cooperation, done in Brussels on 20 December 2012 [2013] OJ L16/2, entered into force on 31 July 2013.

18 Convention for the Unification of Certain Rules Relating to International Carriage by Air, signed at Warsaw on 12 November 1929, LNTS, Vol 137, No 3145, entered into force on 13 February 1933.

and supplemented several times. This act was later complemented by the 1999 Montreal Convention.[19] The Warsaw Convention, as amended, and the Montreal Convention apply simultaneously; however, the latter prevails in relations between states that are parties to this treaty. The Warsaw-Montreal system lays down liability rules for international carriage by air. It also regulates travel documents, air carrier insurance, some other duties related to carriage and jurisdiction matters. The UK is party to both the Warsaw Convention (and all its amendments in force) and the Montreal Convention. The Montreal Convention has also been approved by the EU, acting as a REIO within its competences.[20]

The UK will remain a party to the Warsaw Convention as amended and the Montreal Convention after its withdrawal from the EU. The fact that the Montreal Convention has been entered into by both the UK and the EU, acting within their shared competences, will not disturb the full application of this instrument to the UK post-Brexit. This is because this convention is silent as regards the division of competences between REIOs and their member states. It also does not allow for any reservations or declarations in this respect, nor does it enable a contracting state to be bound by part of its provisions. Therefore, after Brexit the UK will continue to be fully bound by this convention and will not need to take any additional legal steps. However, the EU derived law which extends the scope of application of the Montreal Convention within the EU will be affected by Brexit.[21]

2.5 Aviation security and criminal law conventions

Aviation security and criminal law is a branch of legislation which lies largely in the national competences of the EU member states. This part of law is internationally organised within several treaties, to which the UK is a party, and sometimes even the depositary. The first of these acts, the 1963 Tokyo Convention,[22] deals with unruly passengers and state jurisdiction as to crimes committed onboard aircraft. The 1970 Hague Convention[23] and

---

19 Convention for the Unification of Certain Rules for International Carriage by Air done at Montreal on 28 May 1999, ICAO Doc 9740; UNTS, Vol 2242, No 39917; [2001] OJ L194/39, entered into force on 4 November 2003.

20 At the relevant time, this concerned issues governed by Council Regulation (EC) No 2027/97 of 9 October 1997 on air carrier liability in the event of accidents [1997] OJ L285/1.

21 See also Chapter 12 of this book.

22 Convention on Offences and Certain Other Acts Committed on Board Aircraft, done in Tokyo on 14 September 1963, ICAO Doc 8364; UNTS 704, 10106, entered into force on 4 December 1969.

23 Convention for the Suppression of Unlawful Seizure of Aircraft, signed at The Hague on 16 December 1970, ICAO Doc 8920; UNTS, Vol 860, No 12325, entered into force on

the 1971 Montreal Convention[24] define international crimes including hijacking and other offences against the safety of civil aviation and obligate state-parties to prosecute and punish the perpetrators. They also contain provisions concerning criminal jurisdiction and extradition.

These treaties lie outside EU interest, and neither of these conventions themselves will be relevant in the context of Brexit. However, the previously mentioned issues are not entirely outside the scope of EU competences. The TFEU proclaims that the EU shall be an area of freedom, security and justice (Article 67[1]) and Title V Chapter 4 TFEU includes rules on judicial cooperation in criminal matters. Accordingly, the EU has some derived legislation which may overlap with the issues governed by the above conventions and, despite opt-outs, the UK is currently bound by some parts of this *acquis*.[25] Therefore, Brexit may indirectly influence the application of the criminal air law conventions.[26]

The UK is also a party to one more aviation security convention – the 1991 Convention on the marking of plastic explosives,[27] which will be intact after Brexit.

---

14 October 1971. This convention has been amended by the Protocol Supplementary to the Convention for the Suppression of Unlawful Seizure of Aircraft, done at Beijing on 10 September 2010, ICAO Doc 9959, entered into force on 1 January 2018, not yet ratified in the UK.

24 Convention for the Suppression of Unlawful Acts against the Safety of Civil Aviation, signed at Montreal on 23 September 1971, ICAO Doc 8966; UNTS, Vol 974, No 14118, entered into force on 26 January 1973, as amended by the Protocol for the Suppression of Unlawful Acts of Violence at Airports Serving International Civil Aviation, supplementary to the Convention of 23 September 1971, done at Montreal on 24 February 1988, ICAO Doc 9518; UNTS, Vol 1589, No 14118, entered into force on 6 August 1989. These acts will be superseded by the Convention on the Suppression of Unlawful Acts Relating to International Civil Aviation, done at Beijing on 10 September 2010, ICAO Doc 9960, not in force and yet not ratified in the UK.

25 In particular, Council Framework Decision 2002/584/JHA of 13 June 2002 on the European arrest warrant and the surrender procedures between member states [2002] OJ L190/1.

26 However, see proposed transitional solutions included in Articles 58(1)(b), 168, 60(2) of Draft Withdrawal Agreement of 19 March 2018, TF50 (2018) 35.

27 Convention on the Marking of Plastic Explosives for the Purpose of Detection, done at Montreal on 1 March 1991, ICAO Doc 9571; UNTS, Vol 2122, No 36984, entered into force on 21 June 1998.

Part II

Impact of Brexit on aviation regulatory content

The previous part has indicated which groups of legal acts will be affected or left intact by Brexit. In particular, many legal acts will cease applying to the UK, and to UK-EU27 traffic. These areas will either be governed by the Brexit resistant legal acts, British laws, or will lack any regulation whatsoever. In such cases the emergent legal gaps will need to be filled by British and international lawmakers, a process which will also involve UK-EU27 aviation arrangements.

The aim of this part is to show the impact of the Brexit-transformed legal environment on particular aviation activities. It will be explained how legal changes will translate into practical problems in the industry. Just as in the previous part, in the first place a hard-Brexit scenario will be considered where no deal is reached between the UK and the EU27 or between the UK and third parties as to the matters under discussion (not that there is no deal at all). It will be indicated which of the relevant aviation regulations will stop applying and which of them will stay in place. Where relevant, the role of British legislation preserving EU laws domestically and the recommendations for post-Brexit solutions will be outlined, whereas a possible transition period when current aviation laws could be applied *mutatis mutandis* in or to the UK will generally be left aside.[1]

---

1 These issues will be discussed in detail in Part IV of this book. Where special provisions for the transition period or for continued application of EU law have already been proposed in EU-UK negotiations as of 19 June 2018, this will also be mentioned in footnotes in the present part of the book.

3 Air services

Economic regulation of air services is a crucial area of air transport law. This is the part of aviation regulation which defines the rights and obligations of air carriers in international and domestic air transport. Economic regulation of air services defines if, when, where and how airlines may operate. This area was traditionally regulated by domestic law and by bilateral air services agreements concluded within the Chicago Convention framework. However, with the creation of the EU single air market, this domain has also been comprehensively harmonised at the EU level and additionally regulated in EU-third party agreements. Not surprisingly, key practical problems related to Brexit in aviation will concern this area of law.

Brexit will undermine the legal foundations of air services between the UK and EU27 member states and between the UK and the EU foreign partners.[1] Importantly, of 155 countries linked by aviation agreements with the UK, 44 are through the UK's membership in the EU. This includes 27 EU member states, four EFTA states, six Western Balkan countries (ECAA members) and seven countries with which the EU has signed comprehensive air services agreements (Canada, Georgia, Israel, Jordan, Moldova, Morocco and the US). These 44 countries are estimated to account for 85% of the UK's air traffic,[2] with the EU27 being the UK's single largest destination, representing 49% of passengers and 54% of scheduled commercial flights.

EU air law and the EU-third party agreements will stop applying to the UK after Brexit. UK-relevant air services will rely entirely on British law and on those international arrangements that will survive Brexit. This will

---

1 See Chapter 1 of this book.
2 Airport Operators Association, 'Building a Strong Aviation Partnership with the EU' (*AOA*, 29 March 2017) <www.aoa.org.uk/building-a-strong-aviation-partnership-with-the-eu/> accessed 5 July 2018.

generally lead to submission of these services directly to the Chicago-bilateral system, though some multilateral arrangements will also apply.

3.1 Traffic and transit rights

Traffic rights are the main category of rights which govern air carrier market access. These rights may be defined either as directions of international air services (known as Freedoms of the Air or traffic rights *sensu stricto*), or as routes including eligible points (route rights). There is no global agreement concerning market access, and traffic rights are exchanged between states in air services agreements based on principles established in the Chicago Convention. However, national laws may also involve market access regulations concerning cabotage and distribution of rights to domestic routes among air carriers.

Following the three EU liberalisation packages and subsequent EU legislation, any such restrictions in market access have been removed as regards domestic and international intra-EU air services. Accordingly, EU air carriers are allowed to operate any services and routes within the EU. In this respect, EU law does not make a distinction between scheduled and non-scheduled services and traffic rights, contrary to the Chicago Convention and bilateral air services agreements. EU regulations also overcome the cabotage restrictions. Additionally, traffic rights in the EU and in EU member states' external relations are largely regulated by EU-third party agreements. Some of these agreements extend the EU single air market access principles, whereas others rely on traditional exchange of traffic rights based on reciprocity. These regimes are now fully applicable to the UK and its air carriers.

After Brexit, in UK-EU27 relations British air carriers will cease to be regarded as EU air carriers and will lose all their traffic rights under regulation 1008/2008.[3] At the same time, EU27 airlines will generally keep their EU air carriers status[4] but will lose their traffic rights arising from this regulation in relation to the UK. As regards scheduled air services, the UK carriers will not be able to operate cabotage services (Eighth and Ninth Freedoms of the Air) in the EU27 member states, while the EU27 airlines will be precluded from such services within the UK. The UK carriers will also be unable to operate air services between two EU27 member states

---

3 Regulation (EC) No 1008/2008 of the European Parliament and of the Council of 24 September 2008 on common rules for the operation of air services in the Community [2008] OJ L293/3.

4 Except where Brexit will change the result of the EU ownership and control test. See Chapter 3.2 of this book.

(Seventh Freedom of the Air).[5] As regards the Third–Sixth Freedoms of the Air, their post-Brexit status will depend mainly on the configuration of the revived bilateral air services agreements between the UK and EU27 member states. The restrictive bilateral agreements will be based on route schedules, while the more liberal ones will allow for open access to the Third and Fourth Freedoms. Both types of agreements will generally enable UK air carriers and EU27 member state air carriers to operate services between the territories of the UK and the EU27 member state concerned. Where the bilateral agreement so allows, UK airlines shall also be able to combine such Third and Fourth Freedom traffic supported by two or more bilateral agreements (also those concluded with non-EU states) and translate them into Sixth Freedom traffic via the UK. The airlines of the EU27 member states will be able to do the same via their home states.[6] Some bilateral agreements between the UK and EU27 member states will also allow for Fifth Freedom traffic. However, to be operational, these traffic rights will in any case require the existence of a pair of corresponding bilateral agreements providing for the Fifth Freedom.[7] The transit rights (First and Second Freedoms of the Air) between the UK and EU27 member states will continue to be guaranteed by existing bilateral air services agreements and by the International Air Services Transit Agreement.[8]

The discussion in the preceding paragraph applies also to relations between the UK and the non-EU parties to the EEA agreement, since this agreement incorporates regulation 1008/2008. It is otherwise in the case of UK-Swiss relations. The EU-Swiss aviation agreement has superseded the relevant provisions of the existing bilateral arrangement between Switzerland and the UK as regards traffic rights exchanged in this agreement (i.e. Third–Seventh Freedoms of the Air limited to territories of Switzerland

---

5 Such air traffic rights have normally not been regulated by traditional bilateral air services agreements that will be revived after Brexit. For the revived bilateral agreements, see Chapter 1.5 of this book.

6 Remarkably, in the latter case, pursuant to Article 15(5) of regulation 1008/2008, EU27 air carriers will be able to combine traffic to and from the UK with intra-EU27 traffic notwithstanding the provisions of bilateral agreements between EU27 member states. Such combined services will be subject to different rules on the UK-EU27 segment (bilateral) and the intra-EU27 segment (regulation 1008/2008).

7 Even on the part of EU27 member states, Article 15(5) of regulation 1008/2008 will not automatically support Fifth Freedom traffic between two EU27 member states via a third state (that is, the UK).

8 See also Chapter 2.1 of this book. However, note that this multilateral agreement attributes the Freedoms of the Air to aircraft, not airlines of the contracting parties. This may cause complications for airlines which operate foreign-registered aircraft. Similar problems may arise with regards to the exchange of freedoms between the UK and EU27 member states in some old-type bilateral air services agreements.

and EU member states).[9] This means that after Brexit, the revived bilateral agreement between the UK and Switzerland[10] will provide only for transit rights and Fifth Freedom rights on some agreed routes to and from non-EU member states.[11] At the same time, in EU27-Swiss relations, UK airlines will not be considered community air carriers and will be deprived of any traffic rights. Brexit will have a similar impact on aviation relations with Morocco.[12]

The post-Brexit relations between the UK and the ECAA partners (other than EU27/EEA member states) and between the UK and the CAA partners will again be governed by bilateral agreements, that would be revived in whole. The same applies to relations between the UK and other partners being parties to those EU vertical agreements which are applied provisionally (the US, Canada, Israel, Jordan).[13] This will have following consequences for traffic rights. From the perspective of EU27 air carriers, Brexit will mean the end to Seventh Freedom rights between the UK and the partners' territories (as well as to Fifth Freedom rights, unless otherwise established in the revived UK-EU27 bilateral agreements). British carriers will lose all traffic rights under EU vertical agreements. Any rights in the corresponding UK-third party relations will once again be governed by the old bilateral agreements. This will generally mean a retreat in terms of traffic rights exchange. UK-US relations give the most apparent illustration of this problem. Currently, under the 2007 EU-US agreement, British carriers enjoy unlimited traffic rights on routes from points behind the EU member states[14] via these states and intermediate points to any point or points in the US and beyond. This is supplemented by Seventh Freedom rights between the US and any points for all-cargo services and between the US and points in the ECCA for combination services. US air carriers have been conferred an analogous range of rights.

---

9 Articles 15–16 of the EU-Swiss agreement.
10 Agreement between Switzerland and United Kingdom of Great Britain and Northern Ireland on air services, done in London on 5 April 1950, AS 1951 575; BBl 1949 II 849, entered into force on 8 June 1951, as amended on 1 February 1993, AS 1993 1280.
11 That is the rights which have not been governed by the EU-Swiss agreement and consequently have not been superseded in bilateral agreements by virtue of Article 16 of the EU-Swiss agreement.
12 However, in this case, it is unclear if the revived UK-Moroccan bilateral agreement will even cover transit rights. This is because in the nomenclature of the EU-Morocco agreement traffic rights include transit rights (Article 2). Hence, it may be argued that these rights in bilateral agreements have been terminated by virtue of Article 26 of the EU-Morocco agreement.
13 Provided these agreements are not in force on Exit Day.
14 This extends to Iceland and Norway subject to an additional agreement.

These generous privileges contrast greatly with the old Bermuda II agreement which exchanges transit rights and confines traffic rights only to eligible gateways and end points specified in the route schedule to the agreement. Similar problems will affect traffic between the UK and Canada.[15] The exchange of traffic rights will become a problem after Brexit also in relations with Israel and Jordan; however, these bilateral markets are less significant, at least for the UK.[16]

Importantly, after Brexit, the Freedoms of the Air between the UK and the states belonging to the current EU aviation regime or EU-third party aviation regimes will only be available if foreseen in the existing air services agreements (or in the multilateral transit agreement) made with the UK. Otherwise, post-Brexit air traffic will have to be arranged based on reciprocity and subject to national laws of the UK[17] and its foreign partners. Notably, in this context, the UK is not linked with an air services agreement with each of the states that currently belong to the aforementioned aviation regimes.[18] As regards non-scheduled air services, post-Brexit relations between the UK and those states will also differ depending on the status of the latter in respect of the Multilateral Agreement on Commercial Rights of Non-Scheduled Air Services[19] and the Chicago Convention.[20] Subject to limitations imposed by contracting states, Article 5 of the Chicago Convention provides for the right of non-scheduled operations that is attached to aircraft (not airlines) of the contracting states. The ECAC agreement further extends this right by admitting aircraft registered in ECAC member states and operated by a national of an ECAC member state who is duly authorised by that state to operate non-scheduled services without the limitations envisaged in the Chicago Convention.

---

15 See Agreement between the Government of the United Kingdom of Great Britain and Northern Ireland and the Government of Canada concerning Air Services, signed in Ottawa on 22 June 1988, UKTS 37 (1989), Cm773, entered into force as of the date of signature.

16 For the impact of Brexit on traffic rights in UK-EU27 and UK-third party relations see also: E-M Cronrath and others 'Brexit – Auswirkungen auf den deutschen und europäischen Luftverkehr' (2016) 96 *Wirtschaftsdienst* 675, 675–677; B Humphreys, 'Brexit and Aviation: All Clear Now?' (2016) XV(3) *Aviation & Space Journal* 30, 35–36.

17 However, even the incorporation of EU law into the British domestic regime does not solve traffic rights issues, which are international by nature. Note that any unilateral actions in this respect may only concern cabotage, overflight and landing rights in the accepting state. See also Chapter 18 of this book.

18 For instance, the UK has no bilateral aviation relations with Kosovo or Liechtenstein. These states are also not parties to the International Air Services Transit Agreement. Kosovo is not party to the Chicago Convention. Liechtenstein has no international airport. There is, however, regular non-stop air traffic between the UK and Kosovo.

19 See Chapter 2.2 of this book.

20 Within this group only Kosovo is not party to this convention.

The preceding discussion reveals that in many instances, traffic rights will be severely limited by Brexit. However, the adverse impact of Brexit on these rights does not have equal economic significance to air carriers. Brexit will especially disturb operations based on cabotage, Seventh and Fifth Freedoms. These rights are particularly useful for point-to-point oriented networks and, hence, primarily exercised by low-cost carriers (LCCs). For instance, non-British airlines such as Ryanair, Norwegian and Wizz Air have built a large part of their business on serving routes between the UK and points outside their home countries, including EU27/EAA/ECAA and even third-party destinations. Ryanair, Aer Lingus and Germania also perform cabotage within the UK. At the same time, UK-based easyJet, Flybe and BMI Regional operate between EU27 member states or within these states.[21] These airlines and air services will be the most hurt by Brexit. Not surprisingly, some of these airlines have already taken measures to secure separate air operator certificates (AOCs) in the UK and in EU27 member states.[22] Conversely, the full-service airlines, which rely more on hub-and-spoke networks, may be content with the Third and Fourth Freedom exchange that will be partially secured post-Brexit by the old bilateral agreements. These carriers shall be more concerned only as regards restrictive bilateral agreements like Bermuda II. However, given their incumbent position, they may well consider any restrictions more harmful for their

21 Thirty-five percent of Irish-based Ryanair's flights are to/from/within the UK, 43% of UK-based easyJet's flights and 35–36% of its ASKs are not to/from/within the UK, and over 24% of Hungary-based Wizz Air's ASKs are on routes between the UK and EU27 states other than the home state of the carrier. UK-based BMI Regional offers a large part of its capacity within the EU27. See: E-M Cronrath and others 'Brexit – Auswirkungen auf den deutschen und europäischen Luftverkehr' (2016) 96 *Wirtschaftsdienst* 675, 677–679; L Harper, 'What is at stake for easyJet and Ryanair from Brexit' (*FlightGlobal*, 11 May 2017) <www.flightglobal.com/news/articles/analysis-what-is-at-stake-for-easyjet-and-ryanair-f-436638/> accessed 7 August 2018; K Hofmann, 'BMI Regional considers possible Brexit strategies' (*ATW Plus*, 28 March 2017) <http://atwonline.com/airlines/bmi-regional-considers-possible-brexit-strategies> accessed 15 June 2018; B Humphreys, 'Brexit and Aviation: All Clear Now?' (2016) XV(3) *Aviation & Space Journal* 30, 32–33; Centre for Asia Pacific Aviation, 'Brexit and aviation Part 3: Importance of Asian models and liberalisation moves will be accelerated' (*CAPA*, 28 June 2016) <https://centreforaviation.com/insights/analysis/brexit-and-aviation-part-3-importance-of-asian-models-and-liberalisation-moves-will-be-accelerated-288736> accessed 15 June 2018; R Doganis, 'UK departure opens Pandora's box' (2017) 33(5) *Airline Business* 14.

22 For instance, Wizz Air and Ryanair have applied for a British AOC, whereas easyJet and Thomas Cook have applied for Austrian and Spanish AOCs, respectively. This strategy, however, may be thwarted by the post-Brexit ownership and control rules. Unless the ownership and control rules are liberalised post-Brexit or, at least, the existing rules are grandfathered, those subsidiaries will have to be majority owned and controlled by local interests (see also Chapter 3.3 of this book).

low-cost competitors or possible other new entrants. Consequently, legacy airlines have been relatively confident about Brexit in their releases, and even seem to view the post-Brexit restrictions on the LCC operations as a source of their own advantage. Time will show whether this will turn out to be a win-lose or lose-lose scenario.

3.2 Airline ownership and control

The exercise of traffic rights is subject to airline eligibility criteria. These criteria, which are established in domestic licensing regulations and in air services agreements, traditionally include a requirement that the airline is substantially (majority) owned and effectively controlled by the state which designates it and/or its nationals. This has been replaced within the EU with a community ownership and control standard. To receive an EU air carrier licence under regulation 1008/2008, the airline must be more than 50% owned and effectively controlled by EU member states and/or their nationals. Moreover, it must have its principal place of business in the territory of the EU member state that grants the licence, and must hold a valid AOC issued by a national authority of a member state, by several national authorities of member states acting jointly or by the EASA.[23] This standard has been extended to those EU-third party relations where EU air law is applied (EEA, ECAA, EU-Swiss agreements). It has also been used in EU vertical agreements for airline designations on the part of EU member states. Additionally, the horizontal agreements have substituted this EU standard for the national ownership and control requirements in many of the EU member states' bilateral agreements.[24] Brexit will have a significant impact on this system.

The first consequence concerns licensing rules in the UK and in the EU27 (which here shall also mean other states where EU air law is applied), which is relevant for UK domestic and EU27 internal traffic. As regards the UK,

---

23 The AOC requirement has recently been liberalised by the provisions of regulation (EU) No 2018/1139 of the European Parliament and of the Council of 4 July 2018 on common rules in the field of civil aviation and establishing a European Union Aviation Safety Agency, and amending Regulations (EC) No 2111/2005, (EC) No 1008/2008, (EU) No 996/2010, (EU) No 376/2014 and Directives 2014/30/EU and 2014/53/EU of the European Parliament and of the Council, and repealing Regulations (EC) No 552/2004 and (EC) No 216/2008 of the European Parliament and of the Council and Council Regulation (EEC) No 3922/91 [2018] OJ L 212/1. According to previous provisions, the licence holder needed to have an AOC issued by a national authority of the same member state whose competent licensing authority was responsible for granting, refusing, revoking or suspending the operating licence.

24 See Chapters 1.4–1.5 of this book.

unless regulation 1008/2008 is fully applied in the UK after Brexit, the UK will need to adopt new licensing rules for its airlines.[25] It is possible that in doing so, the UK may choose to adhere to a British ownership and control standard.[26] In such case, carriers other than those which are British majority owned and effectively controlled will not be fit under the new rules, and will be unable to operate within the UK.[27] However, the UK may well decide to keep such airlines operating by admitting unilaterally EU27 ownership and control, by building its licensing regime on the principal place of business criterion (without any reference to ownership and control),[28] or at least by means of grandfathered rights or exemptions.[29] As regards EU27 airlines, absent special post-Brexit aviation arrangements, the British interests in such airlines will be treated as third-party interests, which will change ownership arithmetic and determination of effective control.

25 Regulation 1008/2008 will be incorporated in the UK by virtue of Section 3 of European Union (Withdrawal) Act 2018, 2018 ch 16; however, absent a UK-EU27 aviation arrangement, this regulation will be unworkable in the UK. Therefore, this regulation will likely be amended based on Section 8 of this act. See also Chapter 18 of this book.

26 This may be justified on the grounds that UK licensing rules will need to correspond with the UK's bilateral agreements that will incorporate national ownership and control clauses. However, such traditional reasoning is not entirely convincing. Ultimately, today regulation 1008/2008 does not correspond with such UK-third party bilateral agreements, which does not prevent UK designations of British owned and controlled carriers.

27 Ownership structures of some UK-based airlines may also be disturbed by Brexit. Shareholdings in Norwegian Air UK and Thomson Airways/TUI Airways are held by Norwegian and German holding companies, respectively. Ownership structure may also be problematic in the context of Air France-KLM's planned acquisition of 31% of shares in UK-based Virgin Atlantic. The takeover would result in this carrier being majority owned by non-UK nationals. Also, British Airways may be exposed to problems with ownership and control requirements. On the one hand, it is a 100% owned subsidiary of Spain-based International Airlines Group (IAG) which was formed by BA and Spanish airline Iberia. On the other hand, this holding structure was designed to secure BA's and Iberia's designations in relations with third states which still require national (British/Spanish) ownership and control. This structure has been tried and tested for several years, which makes BA rather confident in this respect, see: Transport Committee, *Oral Evidence: Aviation and Brexit* (HC 531, 30 October 2017) Q4. However, this holding structure has not been tried and tested (did not need to be) in respect of airline licensing rules and UK-EU27 relations. Therefore, some commentators have doubts concerning IAG's post-Brexit status, e.g. SJ Fox, 'Brexit: A Bolt from the Blue! – Red Sky in the Morning?' (2016) 16 *Issues in Aviation Law and Policy* 83, 113–114.

28 A solution already applied in some parts of the world. See J Walulik, *Progressive Commercialization of Airline Governance Culture* (Abingdon, New York: Routledge 2017) 152–162.

29 Notably, prior to the adoption of the EU rules, the UK operating licences were granted to air carriers which were British owned and controlled, unless exempted by the Secretary of State (Section 65(3) of the Civil Aviation Act 1982). See L Vrbaski, 'Flying into the Unknown: The UK's Air Transport Relations with the European Union and Third Countries Following "Brexit"' (2016) 41(6) *Air & Space Law* 421, 424.

This may result in some EU27 carriers being non-eligible under regulation 1008/2008.[30] To protect British investments in EU27 airlines an agreement between the UK and the EU27 would be required.[31] The post-Brexit status of foreign investments in airlines will be inconvenient for both the UK and the EU27; therefore, there is a chance that this situation will trigger liberalisation of ownership and control rules regionally, and perhaps multilaterally in a longer perspective.[32]

As regards the post-Brexit relations between the UK and the EU27 (here including other states where EU aviation law is applied), the ownership and control of designated airlines will be governed by bilateral agreements, provided that they are revived.[33] Unless modified by horizontal agreements,[34] the revived bilateral agreements will generally follow the traditional national ownership and control requirement.[35] Consequently, a UK-based

---

30 This may be the case with IAG. The group has several EU27 based subsidiaries. As mentioned IAG's holding has been designed to secure the status of Iberia as Spanish majority owned and effectively controlled. This however does not apply to other subsidiaries including OpenSkies, Vueling and Aer Lingus. IAG may, therefore, require restructuring due to Brexit. Irish based Ryanair and Hungary based Wizz Air may also fall below the required EU majority ownership threshold when their UK shareholders cease to be EU member state nationals. It was reported that these airlines are considering adjusting their ownership structures. See: B Humphreys, 'Brexit and Aviation: All Clear Now?' (2016) XV(3) *Aviation & Space Journal* 30, 37–38; T McEnaney, 'Blue sky between airlines on Brexit' *The Times* (London, 14 March 2018) 33.

31 Regulation 1008/2008 already makes reservations concerning ownership and control as to agreements with third countries to which the EU is a party (Article 4[f]). However, note that liberalisation of this regulation is also possible. The EU is currently working on some changes to the ownership and control principle to facilitate foreign investment in airlines. See Commission and others, 'An Aviation Strategy for Europe' (Communication) COM/2015/0598 final.

32 Cf L Vrbaski, 'Flying into the Unknown: The UK's Air Transport Relations with the European Union and Third Countries Following "Brexit"' (2016) 41(6) *Air & Space Law* 421, 424–426.

33 All airline nationality clauses in bilateral agreements between the UK and EU27/EEA/ECAA states will be revived, because regulation 1008/2008 has not superseded such clauses. It will be otherwise in UK-Swiss relations, whereby all relevant provisions of the UK-Swiss agreement have been superseded by the EU-Swiss agreement. For the scope of superseded provisions, see also Chapter 1.5 of this book.

34 Note that in the UK's bilateral agreements with Croatia, Bulgaria and Romania, the ownership and control clauses on the part of the UK have been effectively amended by EU horizontal agreements before these three countries became EU member states. The same applies to bilateral aviation relations between the UK and West Balkan ECAA member states. These states have also signed horizontal agreements with the EU that have amended their bilateral agreements with the UK.

35 The ECAC multilateral agreement for non-scheduled flights is more liberal. It attaches rights to aircraft, not airlines, and requires that the aircraft is operated by a national of any of the contracting states.

carrier will only be eligible if majority owned and effectively controlled by the UK and/or its nationals. Any interests held by EU27 member states and/or their nationals will count as foreign.[36] Accordingly, an EU27 member state carrier will qualify if majority owned and effectively controlled by the state concerned or by its nationals. In such case, it is not only the British interests in such an airline which count as foreign, but also interests held by other EU27 member states.[37] Save for a blind-eye policy (bilateral agreements allow the waiving of ownership and control requirements), these problems could generally be solved in a UK-EU27 vertical (or at least horizontal) agreement whereby pre-Brexit ownership and control criteria would be retained for airlines on both sides.[38] Alternatively, the UK and the EU27 may agree for airline eligibility criteria based on principal place of business and effective regulatory control.[39]

In UK-third party relations that are currently governed by EU vertical agreements, the old bilateral agreements will generally be revived after Brexit.[40] However, this will lead to a restoration of bilateral requirements concerning national ownership and control – although only in the UK-US and the UK-Canada air services agreements. The other revived UK bilateral agreements with Georgia, Israel, Jordan and Moldova have been modified by virtue of EU horizontal agreements. Consequently, in UK-US and UK-Canada relations, any UK-based carriers that are not British majority owned and effectively controlled will be deprived of their rights.[41]

Brexit will obviously not impact on airline nationality requirements in those UK bilateral agreements that are still based on traditional ownership

---

36 This may harm the UK-EU27 traffic served by UK based airlines such as Thomson Airways/TUI Airways.
37 For instance, Austrian Airlines, Brussels Airlines and SWISS – wholly owned subsidiaries of German carrier Lufthansa – would not be eligible for designation under the old UK bilateral agreements with Austria, Belgium and Switzerland. Ryanair could face problems with its previously mentioned British shareholdings. Airlines within the Air France/KLM holding may also be at risk, just like the EU27 subsidiaries of the IAG holding, in particular OpenSkies, Vueling and Aer Lingus.
38 Should this be regarded as too liberal, a safeguard may be introduced to ensure that any British shareholdings in EU27 airlines and any EU27 shareholdings in UK air carriers which exceeded their pre-Brexit levels will be treated as third-party shareholdings.
39 Although this solution is less likely, since it makes space for third-party free riding.
40 Except for the UK-Morocco air services agreement of which relevant provisions have been superseded by the agreement between the EU and Morocco. This may also concern some other agreements depending on the date of their entry into force. See Chapter 1.5 of this book.
41 For instance, Norwegian Air UK, Thomson Airways/TUI Airways and Virgin Atlantic all operate services to third countries. As mentioned previously, the non-UK shareholdings of these airlines may become problematic after Brexit.

and control criteria and remain untouched by EU horizontal agreements. It is a different story in relation to UK bilateral agreements which originally contained EU ownership and control clauses or have been amended to include such clauses (in particular, by virtue of EU horizontal agreements). In such cases, the UK-based airlines (i.e. holding British AOC) will cease to be EU air carriers as referred to in these clauses and, notwithstanding their ownership and control structure, will not be eligible for designation by the UK. At the same time, the EU27-based airlines (i.e. holding AOC from EU27 states[42]) will be eligible for designation by the UK, only provided that they are majority owned and effectively controlled by EU27 states and/or their nationals.[43]

As regards EU27-third party relations where EU horizontal and vertical agreements apply, Brexit will not change the EU ownership and control clauses, as such. However, any British AOC holders will not be regarded as EU air carriers post-Brexit and will not be eligible for designation by EU27 member states. Additionally, any UK shareholdings in EU27-based airlines will be regarded as third-party interests. Therefore, some EU27 airlines may fail to meet the ownership and control criteria.[44] The same will apply to those EU27 member states' bilateral agreements with third parties that encompass the standard EU ownership and control clause.[45] These problems can only be fixed by a third-party blind-eye policy or by renegotiation of vertical, horizontal or bilateral agreements by the EU27 and/or its member states.

Finally, Brexit may distress possible UK and US investments in third party airlines. Currently, the 2007 EU-US air transport agreement guarantees that parties to this agreement will not refuse, revoke, suspend or limit authorisations or permissions for airlines of third states, on the grounds that substantial ownership (or, in some instances, effective control) of these airlines is vested in another party (Annex 4, Article 2). This privilege will not apply to the UK and to UK-US aviation relations after Britain withdraws from the EU.

---

42 This shall also include AOCs issued under the new regulation 2018/1139 by national authorities of member states, by several national authorities of member states acting jointly or by the EASA.

43 See also L Vrbaski, 'Flying into the Unknown: The UK's Air Transport Relations with the European Union and Third Countries Following "Brexit"' (2016) 41(6) *Air & Space Law* 421, 426–427.

44 See, e.g. the aforementioned ownership structures of Ryanair, OpenSkies, Vueling or Aer Lingus, which may prevent these airlines from exercising traffic rights in EU27-third party relations.

45 See Chapter 1.5 of this book.

3.3　Other airline rights and obligations

Traffic rights and airline nationality criteria define the types of agreed air services and airlines eligible to operate them. However, air law also governs key parameters of these services, including number of designated airlines, frequency and capacity, tariffs, combining services, code share and other airline cooperative activities as well as other ancillary rights of air carriers.[46] These issues have traditionally been regulated in air services agreements. Prior to the liberalisation, in the EU they were also a part of domestic laws.

Currently these matters are ruled in a liberal manner in EU-derived law, mostly in regulation 1008/2008, and in EU-third party agreements. Brexit will change this legal environment. After regulation 1008/2008 ceases to apply to and in the UK, air carrier rights and obligations in the UK's domestic air services will need to be redefined in British national legislation.[47] As regards air services between the UK and EU27 member states, air carrier rights and obligations will return to being governed by bilateral agreements, with the exception of those restrictions concerning operation of air services that have been superseded by virtue of regulation 1008/2008.[48] Possible air carrier rights and obligations in relations between the UK and other parties will depend on the scope of revived bilateral provisions.[49] It would be impossible to catalogue here all post-Brexit changes in this respect. Selected problems will be discussed ahead.

The EU law admits all EU air carriers to intra-EU services. It does not require a separate act of air carrier designation, nor does it limit the number of operating airlines, frequencies or capacity.[50] In UK-EU27 relations, bilateral restrictions concerning these areas have been superseded by virtue of Article 15(4) clause 2 of regulation 1008/2008, and this shall survive Brexit.[51] The act of designation is also not required in EU vertical air services

---

46　For a digest, see International Civil Aviation Authority, *Manual on the Regulation of International Air Transport* (Doc 9626, ICAO 2004).

47　This will likely be achieved by incorporation of regulation 1008/2008 into the British legal system by virtue of Section 3 of European Union (Withdrawal) Act 2018. Note that the incorporated regulation will only have domestic effect and will require amendments to be operational. See also Chapter 18 of this book.

48　Article 15(4) clause 2 of regulation 1008/2008 has superseded restrictions on operation of air services arising from bilateral agreements between member states. The scope of such superseded restrictions is not entirely clear. See discussion ahead.

49　See Chapter 1.5 of this book.

50　Some operational limitations may be imposed on carriers, but only on a non-discriminatory basis under objective criteria relating to safety, security, the protection of the environment and the allocation of slots (regulation 1008/2008, Articles 19–21).

51　See also Chapter 1.5 of this book.

agreements. However, in UK-third party relations, the post-Brexit revival of old bilateral agreements may restore the requirements for designation and, more importantly, limit the number of airlines which may be designated by a contracting party.[52] The revived agreements will also usually be more restrictive in terms of capacity and frequency than the EU-vertical agreements.[53] Brexit shall be irrelevant for situations whereby an EU horizontal agreement has superseded the UK-third party designation clause along with the limitations included therein. The horizontally introduced EU clause will remain in place.[54] Where the UK's bilateral agreements are revived, Brexit may restore possible restrictions on combining air services and entering code-share arrangements,[55] which may possibly lead to some complications in the functioning of airline alliances.[56] Depending on the revived bilateral provisions, the rules concerning aircraft leasing may also change after Brexit. On the one hand, this may result in retreat when compared to current freedoms. On the other hand, some of the present limitations imposed by regulation 1008/2008 will not apply to UK airlines in bilateral relations after Brexit.[57]

As regards air tariffs, regulation 1008/2008 and EU third-party agreements are based on the free-determination principle. A post-Brexit return to bilateral agreements will often mean reintroduction of restrictive tariff regulations in the UK's relations with EU27 member states[58] and third parties.[59] This may translate into the reintroduction of regulatory price setting factors,

---

52 For instance, Article 3(2) of the Bermuda II agreement introduces limitations on the number of designated air carriers.

53 Cf. Article 3(4) of the EU-US air transport agreement and Article 11(4)–(5) and Annex 2 of the Bermuda II agreement.

54 See also Chapter 1.4.3 of this book.

55 It is debatable whether Article 15(4) clause 2 of regulation 1008/2008 has superseded such restrictions in UK-EU27 bilateral agreements. It seems that the issues of combining air services and code share have been autonomously addressed in Article 15(4) clause 1 and in Article 15(5) of the regulation and there is no reason why Article 15(4) clause 2 would need to cover them.

56 However, bilateral agreements have generally been liberal in these areas.

57 See Chapter 11 of this book.

58 As regards UK-EU27 relations, it is unclear which bilateral provisions on tariffs will be revived post-Brexit and which have been effectively superseded. Article 22(2) of regulation 1008/2008 speaks of superseding only the *remaining* restrictions on pricing arising from bilateral agreements between EU member states, including with respect to routes to third countries. It seems that the *remaining* restrictions are restrictions other than those already overruled by the preceding clauses of Article 22 (emphasis added).

59 Bilateral agreements concluded in line with regulation 847/2004, and bilateral agreements amended by EU horizontal agreements will continue to include standard EU pricing clauses which submit airline tariffs to EU law. However, these clauses concern only carriage wholly within the EU, which will make them generally inoperative after Brexit.

mandatory tariff consultations between airlines and a system of adminis-trative tariff approvals. These kinds of arrangements are included e.g. in the Bermuda II agreement (Article 12) and in the ECAC sponsored 1967 International Agreement on the Procedure for the Establishment of Tariffs for Scheduled Air Services.[60] However, as already mentioned, tariff consul-tations will not be allowed in UK-EU27 relations, since they would be in breach of EU competition rules. Finally, regulation 1008/2008 incorporates some non-discrimination provisions and information obligations concern-ing fares and rates, that will not apply to the UK after Brexit.

Brexit may also disturb various types of air carrier ancillary or doing business rights concerning ground-handling, intermodal services, sales and marketing, CRS, employment of non-national personnel, currency conver-sion, etc. Within the EU, such rights are generally attributed to EU airlines, thanks to the Treaty freedoms. Additionally, EU law embraces some avia-tion-specific rules in this respect, especially in the areas of airline self-han-dling[61] and non-discriminatory access to CRS.[62] This system extends to the non-EU states where EU air law is applied. Ancillary rights have also been regulated in a liberal manner in the EU vertical agreements.[63] After Brexit, air carrier ancillary rights in the UK and their relations with aviation part-ners will be subject only to UK laws and to the UK's bilateral air services agreements, provided that they are revived. This may lead to some restraints in airline commercial opportunities and to the disappearance of some regu-latory safeguards. However, the impact of Brexit on these privileges will not be as significant as in respect of other air carrier rights. Bilateral agreements usually involve provisions on ancillary rights,[64] and some airline commercial opportunities concerning sales and marketing of air transport services and CRS can also be guaranteed by the GATS system. The EU has made some commitments as regards market access and national treatment in these areas and they will survive Brexit. Access to the UK market through GATS will depend on the UK's post-Brexit schedules of commitments.[65]

---

60 See Chapter 2.2 of this book.
61 Council Directive 96/67/EC of 15 October 1996 on access to the groundhandling market at Community airports [1996] OJ L272/36.
62 Regulation (EC) No 80/2009 of the European Parliament and of the Council of 14 Janu-ary 2009 on a Code of Conduct for computerised reservation systems and repealing Coun-cil Regulation (EEC) No 2299/89 [2009] OJ L35/47.
63 See, e.g. Articles 10 and 17 of the EU-US air transport agreement.
64 In particular, bilateral agreements concluded in line with regulation 847/2004 must intro-duce a standard EU clause on ground-handling.
65 See also Chapter 1.6 of this book.

Another part of air services regulations that will stop applying to the UK after Brexit is the Public Service Obligation (PSO) rules contained in regulation 1008/2008.[66] The UK has used this regulation to establish numerous scheduled air services to peripheral regions of its territory. To maintain these services operating after Brexit, the UK will need to introduce national instruments aimed at providing essential air connectivity.[67]

---

66 However, according to preliminarily agreed interim provisions, public procurement procedures under Articles 16, 17 and 18 of regulation 1008/2008 shall be continued if launched before the end of the transition period and not yet finalised on the last day thereof. See Article 72 of Draft Withdrawal Agreement of 19 March 2018, TF50 (2018) 35.

67 Once again, simple incorporation of regulation 1008/2008 into the British legal regime based on Section 3 of European Union (Withdrawal) Act 2018 seems insufficient.

4 Airport services

Airport services are regulated at the EU level; however, unlike air services, EU economic regulation in this respect is not comprehensive and concerns only some selected airport activities. The EU airport laws are addressed to certain categories of airports within the EU and are relevant in the context of any air services operated from such airports. Brexit will bring about two categories of problems in respect of airport regulation. The first will concern possible legal gaps as regards regulation of British airport activities. The second will be connected with non-discriminatory access to airport services in UK-EU27 relations.

The primary EU legal instrument dedicated to airports is the directive on airport charges.[1] It sets common principles for charges related to landing, take-off, lighting and parking of aircraft and processing of passengers and freight. These principles are applicable at each member state's airport with the highest passenger movement, and at any other airports with an annual traffic over five million passenger movements. The scope of the directive is rather modest. It requires that member states ensure that charges do not discriminate among airport users and that regular and transparent consultations are held between the airport managing body and airport users. Brexit shall have little practical impact in this area. On the UK part, the directive will cease to apply; however, this will not automatically nullify national laws which implement it.[2] On the EU27's part, there will be no changes. Even though the directive's non-discrimination principle refers to EU law, it seems unlikely that the UK or the EU27 could discriminate against each other in terms of airport charges after exit from the EU. In the end, Article 15 of the Chicago Convention prohibits any discrimination in airport charges.[3]

1 Directive 2009/12/EC of the European Parliament and of the Council of 11 March 2009 on airport charges [2009] OJ L70/11.
2 These will be 'saved' by Section 2 of European Union (Withdrawal) Act 2018, 2018 ch 16.
3 Although this is with regard to the nationality of aircraft, not of airport users.

Another airport activity which is dealt with by EU derived law is ground-handling.[4] The ground-handling directive 96/67[5] encompasses detailed provisions applicable to several categories of airports in the EU. This covers access to the ground-handling market and to self-handling, procedures for selection of service suppliers, access to airport infrastructure, financial transparency and consultations with airport users. The directive has led to the development of a third-party ground-handling market across the EU served by suppliers independent from airlines. The directive was transposed to EU member states' legal systems, and Brexit alone will not rescind that.[6] Brexit may, however, have impact on the access of British providers to EU27 ground-handling markets, and *vice versa*. In these relations, Article 15 of the Chicago Convention can partly secure an airline's position after Brexit.[7] Remarkably, the EU directive does not preclude third-state suppliers from access to the EU ground-handling market (or third-state airport users from access to self-handling). It only allows limiting this access if the third states concerned do not offer reciprocal benefits to EU suppliers or airport users. This points to possible post-Brexit ground-handling arrangements between the UK and EU27 member states.

The third area of airport activities that is harmonised at the EU level is the allocation of slots. Regulation 95/93[8] organises a system of allocation of times of arrival or departure at coordinated EU airports. This system is aimed to offer non-discriminatory access to slots and to balance the interests

---

4 Also, EU vertical agreements and EU standard clauses for member states' bilateral agreements involve ground-handling provisions. However, they concentrate on air carrier rights concerning ground-handling, not on ground-handling services as such.

5 Directive 96/67/EC of the Council of 15 October 1996 on access to the groundhandling market at Community airports, [1996] OJ L272/36.

6 Also instructive in this regard are preliminarily agreed interim provisions on public procurement procedures under Articles 11 and 12 of the directive included in Article 72 of Draft Withdrawal Agreement of 19 March 2018, TF50 (2018) 35. Mutual compliance with the non-discrimination principle in respect of public procurement has also been preliminarily agreed; see 'Joint statement from the negotiators of the European Union and the United Kingdom Government on progress of negotiations under Article 50 TEU on the United Kingdom's orderly withdrawal from the European Union', 19 June 2018, TF50 (2018) 52. However, it is worth pointing out that these rules are genuinely 'interim' in the sense that they only govern procedures launched before the end of the transition period and not yet finalised on the last day thereof (31 December 2020).

7 It establishes that every airport in a contracting state which is open to public use by its national aircraft shall likewise, subject to the provisions of Article 68 of the convention, be open under uniform conditions to the aircraft of all the other contracting states. This rule may be construed as guaranteeing non-discriminatory provision of ground-handling and non-discriminatory access to self-handling.

8 Council Regulation (EEC) No 95/93 of 18 January 1993 on common rules for the allocation of slots at Community airports OJ L14/1.

of incumbent airlines with new entrants. The regulation does not distinguish between EU air carriers and third-party air carriers. Airports are designated as coordinated when slot or capacity problems occur or when member states consider it necessary.[9] On Exit Day, regulation 95/93 will in reality cease to apply to UK airports; however, it will be converted into UK law by the European Union (Withdrawal) Act. This will be relevant to British, EU27 and third-party users of these airports. In EU27 member states, the regulation will be fully applicable, including to UK air carriers. Notably, there are no international rules for slot allocation.[10] Post-Brexit, congestion problems at UK airports will be solved directly by British lawmakers. Despite some calls for more flexible and commercial slot distribution schemes,[11] in practice the UK will be limited in regulating slots independently from the EU even in the case of a hard Brexit. If the UK does not grant EU27 air carriers treatment comparable to that granted by EU27 member states to UK air carriers subject to regulation 95/93 or will not grant EU27 carriers de facto national treatment, UK air carriers may be deprived of protection under regulation 95/93 in the EU27.[12] Brexit may also indirectly hurt the British slot coordinator which has been designated in EU27 member states under regulation 95/93.[13] Although these designations will remain valid, the lack of Treaty freedoms may have an adverse impact on the overseas activity of the coordinator.

A similar post-Brexit mechanism may also work against other airport-related activities in the UK and the EU27. Currently such services, even if unregulated by EU-derived law, are subject to the Treaty freedoms. For instance, unlike airline ownership, EU law does not directly control airport ownership. Many EU airports have been privatised, and trans-national ownership is not uncommon in this sector.[14] Not least, there have been UK investments in EU27 airports and *vice versa.*[15] Presently such investments

---

9 Currently in the UK, all airports serving London (Heathrow, Gatwick, Stansted, Luton and City) and Manchester airport are coordinated.

10 There are, however, international guidelines published by IATA. See International Air Transport Association, *Worldwide Slot Guidelines* (8th edn, IATA 2017).

11 See A Haylen and L Butcher, *Airport slots* (House of Commons Library Briefing Paper No CBP 488, 12 June 2017) 25.

12 See Article 12 of regulation 95/93.

13 ACL, a UK based slot-coordination company, has been designated at several EU27 airports in Ireland, Poland and Luxemburg.

14 See Airports Council International, *The Ownership of Europe's Airports 2016* (ACI Europe 2017).

15 See 'Airport investment: The top 10 investors from CAPA's Global Airport Investors Database' (*CAPA*, 9 August 2017) <https://centreforaviation.com/insights/analysis/airport-investment-the-top-10-investors-from-capas-global-airport-investors-database-360459> accessed 10 June 2018.

are sheltered by the principle of free movement of capital between EU member states. After Brexit, their admissibility will rely only on the national laws of the UK and EU27 member states. Where these laws require majority national (or EU/EEA) shareholdings in airports, the trans-border investments may upset post-Brexit airport ownership arithmetic, just as in the case of airlines.

Airports will also be indirectly influenced by the impact of Brexit on traffic rights.[16] Some airports are largely or even mostly (e.g. Belfast City, London Stansted) reliant on Seventh Freedom traffic within the EU. When such traffic will stop being supported post-Brexit, these airports may lose an important part of their business. The impact of Brexit on airline ownership and control[17] may bring about similar results for airports where the Brexit-affected air carriers are now based.

On Exit Day, the UK will also be outside the EU customs union, which means that customs borders will be restored between the UK and EU. This will have effect in particular on British airports where a large part of the now customs-free traffic will be subjected to additional procedures.[18] Similar problems may concern immigration and security controls if these procedures become more stringent with reference to EU27 citizens after Brexit. These issues may seriously impede the functioning of many UK airports. UK authorities will need to provide new staffing and introduce legislative and organisational solutions to mitigate the negative outcomes. There is some consolation for UK airports in the fact that the return of customs borders may also mean reintroduction of duty free for European flights.[19]

16 See Chapter 3.1 of this book.
17 See Chapter 3.2 of this book.
18 It is estimated that the EU27 accounts for 47% of British exports and 54% of imports, see A Goodwin, 'Brexit – Customs borders will impose costs and delays' (2017) 41(2) *Economic Outlook* 11.
19 B Humphreys, 'Brexit and Aviation: All Clear Now?' (2016) XV(3) *Aviation & Space Journal* 30, 40.

5 Fair competition

There is no universal framework for securing fair competition in the aviation sector. The EU was the first to develop an advanced trans-national system of competition laws to support undisturbed operation of its internal market. This arrangement, which is currently based on the TFEU provisions[1] and cross-sector derived law,[2] applies directly to the EU aviation market and even to third-party actions which have an impact on this market. EU competition law is based on: 1) prohibition of agreements or concerned practices between undertakings that may affect trade between EU member states by preventing, restricting or distorting competition; 2) prohibition of abuse of dominant position; 3) control of concentrations between undertakings; and 4) prohibition of any kind of state aid distorting competition. The EU aviation industry, including air carriers, airports and airline manufacturers, is entirely subject to this system.

Theory suggests that this system will not apply to the UK, to UK-EU27 relations or to UK-third party relations after Brexit, because the UK will be outside the scope of the Treaties and the derived law. This is true, although as already mentioned, the application of EU competition law extends to any actions that have an impact on the EU internal market. Therefore, UK airlines will still need to abide by this law in many respects. For instance, price setting and exercise of some ancillary rights (e.g. concerning code share) on UK-EU27 routes will have to comply with European competition rules even after Brexit. Notwithstanding airline nationality, any air carrier concentrations that have an EU dimension will remain subject to EU competition law. This may involve not only trans-national concentrations in UK-EU27 relations, but also those entirely within the UK. Importantly, on Exit Day,

1 Articles 101–109.
2 In particular, Council Regulation (EC) No 139/2004 of 20 January 2004 on the control of concentrations between undertakings [2004] OJ L24/1.

the UK will lose its impact on the shape of EU competition law or on its enforcement – that will remain with the EU27.[3] This situation will have a significant influence on airlines and their alliances. In particular the three strategic mega-alliances (oneworld, Star Alliance, Sky Team) have all received competition clearance from the European Commission. The Commission has also imposed some commitments on alliance participants. After Brexit, these resolutions may partly lose their legal foundation because some airline activities and air services will fall outside the scope of EU air law, EU vertical agreements and EU competition law. This may upset the European Commission's competences and its calculations concerning the impact of alliances on the EU internal market, which as a result may undermine the alliance clearance.

In UK-third party relations the removal of EU vertical agreements will also affect competition clauses.[4] What is more, the revival of previous bilateral agreements may have negative consequences for competition clearance by third state authorities. Notably, the US Department of Transportation (DOT) has been ready to immunise international airline alliances from the US antitrust laws only if these alliances operate within open skies regimes. This was a precondition for the grant of transatlantic antitrust immunities to the three global strategic alliances. The substitution of the liberal EU-US air transport agreement with the restrictive Bermuda II agreement will eliminate the key justification for antitrust immunities in UK-US relations. This will hit the previously mentioned alliances hard – in particular oneworld, which includes British Airways. It seems, thus, that a post-Brexit UK-US open skies arrangement will be necessary to ensure uninterrupted operation of these alliances.

Notwithstanding the competition provisions in horizontal and vertical EU aviation agreements and in bilateral air services agreements, the EU has concluded with third parties a number of cross-sector agreements dedicated to fair competition. The treaties with key economic partners set rules for cooperation on the application of competition laws which apply also to EU member states' competition authorities.[5] On Exit Day, these arrangements

---

3 However, as regards competition enforcement, absent any post-Brexit arrangement, it will be problematic for the European Commission to carry out investigations in the UK.

4 At the same time, competition clauses introduced in the UK's bilateral agreements by virtue of EU horizontal agreements will still be in place; however, these bilateral agreements will not cover UK air carriers. See Chapter 1.5 of this book.

5 These agreements provide for a mechanism of information exchange between the EU member states' competition authorities (via the European Commission) and third-party authorities. Other types of EU agreements on competition issues are memoranda between the European Commission and third-party antitrust authorities which do not pertain to member state authorities.

will stop covering UK authorities, which may contribute to less effective enforcement of British competition laws in air transport and in other areas of civil aviation.

Finally, if EU competition law is under discussion, then mention should be made of the state aid rules. Article 107 TFEU prohibits aid granted by a member state or through state resources in any form whatsoever, which distorts or threatens to distort competition by favouring certain undertakings or the production of certain goods and affects trade between member states. This law has been widely applied to air carriers, airports and aircraft manufacturers across the EU. Additionally, provisions concerning subsidies have been implemented in EU vertical agreements, although without precise definition of prohibited practices. After Brexit, the UK will be outside this system. The primary consequence is that the UK will no longer be confined by the EU legal straitjacket. However, how the UK government will utilise its recovered freedom is important. First, it is doubtful whether the absence of state aid control will be a proper foundation on which to build a sound national free-market aviation policy.[6] Second, it is unlikely that the EU would agree to any post-Brexit deal with the UK that would disregard fair competition issues including state aid. Therefore, it seems that despite Brexit, the UK will remain influenced by the EU regime in this respect.

---

6 Cf. A Biondi, 'The First on the Flight Home: The Sad Story of State Aid Control in the Brexit Age' (2016) 27 *King's Law Journal* 442.

6 Aviation safety

Technical requirements in aviation have been directly harmonised at the EU level in order to establish a high uniform level of safety. This *acquis* has been generally organised within framework regulation 2018/1139[1] and the accompanying European Commission regulations which govern a wide range of issues including airworthiness specifications, certification and continued airworthiness, requirements and administrative procedures related to aircrew, air traffic controllers, air operations, aerodromes, common rules of the air and operational provisions regarding services and procedures in air navigation, common airspace usage requirements and operating procedures for airborne collision avoidance, and common requirements for the provision of air navigation services, safety oversight in air traffic management and air navigation services.[2] Within this system, the European Union Aviation Safety Agency (EASA)[3] has been established to assist the European Commission in preparing regulations and to issue specifications and guidance material thereto. EASA also works, exclusively or together with

---

1 Regulation (EU) No 2018/1139 of the European Parliament and of the Council of 4 July 2018 on common rules in the field of civil aviation and establishing a European Union Aviation Safety Agency, and amending Regulations (EC) No 2111/2005, (EC) No 1008/2008, (EU) No 996/2010, (EU) No 376/2014 and Directives 2014/30/EU and 2014/53/EU of the European Parliament and of the Council, and repealing Regulations (EC) No 552/2004 and (EC) No 216/2008 of the European Parliament and of the Council and Council Regulation (EEC) No 3922/91 [2018] OJ L 212/1.

2 The accompanying European Commission regulations that are still based on the previous framework regulation (EC) No 216/2008 of the European Parliament and of the Council of 20 February 2008 on common rules in the field of civil aviation and establishing a European Aviation Safety Agency, and repealing Council Directive 91/670/EEC, Regulation (EC) No 1592/2002 and Directive 2004/36/EC [2008] OJ L79/1 shall be adapted to the new framework regulation 2018/1139 by 12 September 2023.

3 Known as European Aviation Safety Agency under previous regulation 216/2008.

member states, as an executive body responsible for the endorsement of the preceding rules.[4]

After its withdrawal from the EU, the UK will not be sheltered by this regulatory system, nor by any of the future EU safety and technical laws. Due to the wide scope of this system, the emergent legal gap will adversely impact any type of aviation activity in the UK, including air transport, general aviation and aircraft manufacturing.[5] Pan-EU validity of certificates of airworthiness, aircrew, air traffic controllers or air operator credentials, together with the Treaty freedoms, has led to internationalisation of aviation industrial activities and the aviation labour market in the EU. The departure of the UK from this framework will lead to technical and legal barriers that may harm the aviation industry and also jeopardise safety on both sides of the English Channel.

The UK and EU27 member states will remain parties to the Chicago Convention. Therefore, safety and technical issues will still be governed by the annexes to this convention after Brexit. However, these annexes establish only the minimum standards in international civil aviation. What is more, they are not automatically binding upon the aviation industry and require implementation into national legal orders, which at the moment is largely accomplished through EU law. After Brexit, the UK will need to adopt new measures to safeguard the full implementation of these international standards.[6] This may be achieved by a UK-EU27 arrangement for the extended application of the EU aviation safety and technical legacy, or by adoption of new British national regulations. Notably, the latter option may be problematic for the UK. Whereas simple incorporation of EU aviation safety laws in the UK[7] will fill the gap in the short run, it must be acknowledged that key institutional resources for the development of such future regulations have been allocated to the EU, and it may be prohibitively expensive and time-consuming for London to replicate them. What is more, it is unlikely that that the UK would be able to handle aviation safety issues without any arrangement with the EU27. In particular, an agreement for mutual acceptance of various technical approvals between the UK and the EU27 would be welcome, because there is currently no legal instrument which could support such a mechanism. The 1960 ECAC agreement on certificates of airworthiness of imported aircraft deals only with certificates of airworthiness of aircraft and does not link the UK with all EU27 member states.

---

4 For institutional post-Brexit matters concerning EASA activity, see Chapter 15 of this book.
5 For the impact of Brexit on aircraft manufacturing see Chapter 10 of this book.
6 Or opt out from some standards, pursuant to Article 38 of the Chicago Convention.
7 See Chapter 18 of this book.

There are also other EU aviation safety provisions outside the regulation 2018/1139 framework that will be hit by Brexit. Subject to regulation 2111/2005,[8] the EU bans some air carriers from operating in the territories of the member states on safety grounds. The lists of banned carriers are updated by the European Commission. This regulation also requires that upon reservation, the air carriage contractor informs passengers of the identity of the operating air carrier, even if the carriage takes place outside the EU. Unless the UK adopts its own measures that would replace the regulation, British passengers will be deprived of this protection and the banned air carriers may be able to operate to and from the UK after it leaves the EU.[9] Brexit will bring no changes to the application of regulation 2111/2005 in the EU27.

Reporting and analysis of occurrences, as well as investigation and prevention of accidents and incidents in civil aviation, are harmonised at the EU level. Regulation 376/2014[10] institutes mandatory and voluntary systems for reporting occurrences and includes safeguards to protect the source of information. It also governs analysis, collection and storage of information at the member state and EU levels and the exchange of information between member states and EASA. Regulation 996/2010[11] embraces comprehensive rules for accident and incident investigation in the EU. It requires cooperation between member state authorities, defines the rights of EASA and member states' authorities to participate in safety investigations and establishes the European Network of Civil Aviation Safety Investigation Authorities. Absent a UK-EU27 post-Brexit arrangement, cooperation between the UK and EU27 member states concerning reporting occurrences and accident and incident investigation will be ruled by Annex 13 and partly by

---

8 Regulation (EC) No 2111/2005 of the European Parliament and of the Council of 14 December 2005 on the establishment of a Community list of air carriers subject to an operating ban within the Community and on informing air transport passengers of the identity of the operating air carrier, and repealing Article 9 of Directive 2004/36/EC [2005] OJ L344/15.

9 Although incorporated into the British legal system by virtue of Section 3 of European Union (Withdrawal) Act 2018, 2018 ch 16 (see Chapter 18 of this book), regulation 2111/2005 will be unworkable in the UK after Brexit since it delegates powers to the European Commission.

10 Regulation (EU) No 376/2014 of the European Parliament and of the Council of 3 April 2014 on the reporting, analysis and follow-up of occurrences in civil aviation, amending Regulation (EU) No 996/2010 of the European Parliament and of the Council and repealing Directive 2003/42/EC of the European Parliament and of the Council and Commission Regulations (EC) No 1321/2007 and (EC) No 1330/2007 [2014] OJ L122/18.

11 Regulation (EU) No 996/2010 of the European Parliament and of the Council of 20 October 2010 on the investigation and prevention of accidents and incidents in civil aviation and repealing Directive 94/56/EC [2010] OJ L295/35.

Annex 19 to the Chicago Convention, just as in the case of UK-third party relations. Provisions of these annexes will substitute only for a small part of the current EU cooperative measures, to the disadvantage of European aviation safety.

Safety issues have also been addressed in some of the EU-third party agreements, which will cease to bind the UK after Brexit. As already mentioned, the EU has entered into agreements with the US, Canada and Brazil to protect reciprocal recognition of technical approvals and to facilitate aviation safety cooperation.[12] After Brexit, the UK will not benefit from these arrangements, and will likely have to negotiate new aviation safety agreements or renegotiate the existing ones.

---

12 See Chapter 1.4.4 of this book.

7 Aviation security

The aviation security law applicable to EU member states is based on several groups of legal acts. The primary role is played by framework regulation 300/2008[1] supplemented and implemented by European Commission regulations. This system establishes common standards and procedures concerning screening of passengers, cabin baggage, hold baggage, cargo, mail and airport supplies, airport access, control and surveillance, aircraft security checks and searches, staff recruitment and training. Member states, air operators and airports are required to endorse security programmes. Member states must also designate authorities competent for aviation security and national quality control programmes. This system ensures recognition of security standards within the EU.

Pursuant to regulation 300/2008, the EU has also entered into agreements with third parties for the recognition of security screening rules at airports. These agreements allow for one-stop security between the third countries and EU member states, which means that passengers, baggage and cargo do not need to be subjected again to security controls when transferring. Regulation 300/2008 has also allowed the EU to sign a security memorandum with the ICAO whereby the EU inspects member states' compliance with ICAO security standards on behalf of the ICAO.[2]

This system, including the regulation 300/2008 framework and international agreements, will not apply to and in the UK after Brexit. The UK will still be bound by ICAO aviation security standards arising from Annex 17 to the Chicago Convention. However, these standards require implementation at national level, which is generally provided in EU member states by

1 Regulation (EC) No 300/2008 of the European Parliament and of the Council of 11 March 2008 on common rules in the field of civil aviation security and repealing Regulation (EC) No 2320/2002 [2008] OJ L97/72.
2 See Chapter 1.4.4 of this book.

means of the regulation 300/2008 framework. Hence, after Brexit, the UK will need to implement ICAO standards on its own.[3] UK will also be subject directly to ICAO security inspections, since it will not be covered by the EU-ICAO audit memorandum. If UK-EU27 traffic is to continue to be governed by a one-stop security principle, the UK will also need a post-Brexit security agreement with the EU.

One another group of Brexit-affected security provisions are the PNR rules. Collecting PNR data has been harmonised in the EU by means of directive 2016/681.[4] PNR data are collected on extra-EU flights (and intra-EU flights if a member state so decides) and processed for prevention, detection, investigation and prosecution of terrorist offences and serious crime. Air carriers shall submit such data to passenger information units established in each member state. The directive contains rules for data protection and its exchange between member states as well as for transfer of data to third countries (on a case-by-case basis) and to Europol. General transfer of PNR data to third countries is governed by separate agreements concluded by the EU with the US, Canada and Australia.[5]

After Brexit the above PNR rules will cease to apply to and in the UK.[6] The UK will be free to manage PNR data processing on its own, setting standards below or over the current level of data protection. Notwithstanding its domestic laws, the UK would also have an interest in facilitating international exchange of PNR data with EU27 member states and third parties, and the latter will likely be seeking such exchange too. The new British legislation and international arrangements will have to accommodate these needs. For these reasons, it seems that the UK will not be entirely free to regulate PNR data processing. In particular if it wishes to exchange this data with EU27 member states based on the provisions of directive

---

3 Incorporation of the regulation 300/2008 framework into British law by virtue of Section 3 of European Union (Withdrawal) Act 2018, 2018 ch 16 (see Chapter 18 of this book), will only temporarily solve this problem. Just as in the case of aviation safety, it will be very difficult for the UK to rebuild its competences in the aviation security area, see Chapter 6 of this book.

4 Directive (EU) 2016/681 of the European Parliament and of the Council of 27 April 2016 on the use of passenger name record (PNR) data for the prevention, detection, investigation and prosecution of terrorist offences and serious crime [2016] OJ L119/132.

5 See Chapter 1.4.4 of this book.

6 However the EU has proposed that in the UK, as well as in the EU27 member states in situations involving the UK, directive 2016/681 shall apply in respect of requests received before the end of the transition period by the passenger information unit in accordance with Articles 9 and 10 of that directive. See Article 59(g) of Draft Withdrawal Agreement of 19 March 2018, TF50 (2018) 35.

2016/681 or possibly on a dedicated UK-EU27 PNR agreement, it will have to establish data protection standards that would be acceptable to the EU.

Finally, some aviation security matters are the subject of multilateral international agreements, which will survive Brexit. These are the aviation security and criminal law conventions: the 1963 Tokyo Convention, the 1970 Hague Convention and the 1971 Montreal Convention.[7]

7 See Chapter 2.5 of this book.

8   Environment protection

Environmental issues are addressed in EU air law at several levels. First, framework regulation 2018/1139[1] and supplementing acts ensure compliance of aviation products, parts and non-installed equipment with environmental protection requirements arising from ICAO standards set forth in Annex 16 to the Chicago Convention. Falling out of this system, the UK will need to implement respective standards on its own. Second, where a noise problem has been identified at an EU airport according to directive 2002/49[2] and the legislation applicable in a member state, the member state concerned shall follow procedures for the introduction of noise-related operating restrictions established in regulation 598/2014.[3] The operating restrictions may include setting a cap on movements or noise quotas, prohibiting additional movements or operations by a specific type of aircraft (e.g. withdrawal from operations of marginally compliant aircraft) or drawing a distinction between daytime measures and night-time measures. After Brexit, regulation 598/2014 will cease to apply to and in the UK,

1 Regulation (EU) No 2018/1139 of the European Parliament and of the Council of 4 July 2018 on common rules in the field of civil aviation and establishing a European Union Aviation Safety Agency, and amending Regulations (EC) No 2111/2005, (EC) No 1008/2008, (EU) No 996/2010, (EU) No 376/2014 and Directives 2014/30/EU and 2014/53/EU of the European Parliament and of the Council, and repealing Regulations (EC) No 552/2004 and (EC) No 216/2008 of the European Parliament and of the Council and Council Regulation (EEC) No 3922/91 [2018] OJ L 212/1.
2 Directive 2002/49/EC of the European Parliament and of the Council of 25 June 2002 relating to the assessment and management of environmental noise – Declaration by the Commission in the Conciliation Committee on the Directive relating to the assessment and management of environmental noise [2002] OJ L 189/12.
3 Regulation (EU) No 598/2014 of the European Parliament and of the Council of 16 April 2014 on the establishment of rules and procedures with regard to the introduction of noise-related operating restrictions at Union airports within a Balanced Approach and repealing Directive 2002/30/EC [2014] OJ L 173/65.

and Britain will need to decide on the existing restrictions and on possible ways to apply or replace the regulation. Theoretically, this regulation will be unilaterally incorporated into the British legal system by means of the European Union (Withdrawal) Act 2018.[4] However, without a UK-EU27 post-Brexit arrangement, the European Commission and EU27 member states will likely lose their right under regulation 598/2014 to have a say on restrictions imposed in the UK. Conversely, the UK will lose its rights in respect of EU27 member states' decisions.

Directive 2008/101[5] has submitted the aviation sector to the EU emissions trading system (EU ETS)[6] whereby a general emissions cap is established within which companies receive or buy tradable emission allowances which they later need to surrender against their individual emissions.[7] Save for legislative amendments that will be required in the UK, the member state national laws implementing the EU ETS in aviation will generally be left intact by Brexit. However, without a special post-Brexit UK-EU27 arrangement, the UK will not be able to participate in the EU ETS scheme, including the transfer and recognition of allowances between the UK and the EU27. The European Commission has already adopted a regulation to safeguard the integrity of the EU ETS when EU law ceases to apply in the UK.[8] This measure regulates marking and restricting the surrender of allowances issued by the UK. It does not concern allowances created for 2018, provided that EU law does not yet cease to apply in the UK by 30 April 2019 or that the surrender of allowances takes place by 15 March 2019.[9] The UK has adopted corresponding rules.[10]

---

4 European Union (Withdrawal) Act 2018, 2018 ch 16. See Chapter 18 of this book.
5 Directive 2008/101/EC of the European Parliament and of the Council of 19 November 2008 amending Directive 2003/87/EC as to include aviation activities in the scheme for greenhouse gas emission allowance trading within the Community [2009] OJ L8/3.
6 The EU ETS was established by virtue of directive 2003/87/EC of the European Parliament and of the Council of 13 October 2003 establishing a scheme for greenhouse gas emission allowance trading within the Community and amending Council Directive 96/61/EC [2003] OJ L275/32.
7 Initially, all airlines operating to, from and within the EU were required to monitor, report and verify their emissions and to surrender allowances against these emissions. This raised disputes with third states which has led the EU to a 'stop-the-clock' decision limiting the scope of the EU ETS to flights within the EU/EEA until 31 December 2023.
8 Commission Regulation (EU) 2018/208 of 12 February 2018 amending Regulation (EU) No 389/2013 establishing a Union Registry [2018] OJ L39/3.
9 See also EU proposal for the transition period included in Article 92(2) of Draft Withdrawal Agreement of 19 March 2018, TF50 (2018) 35.
10 The Greenhouse Gas Emissions Trading Scheme (Amendment) Regulations 2017, SI 2017/1207.

Even if the UK will not participate in the EU ETS after Brexit, given the UK's position concerning climate change policy, it is unlikely that Britain will not continue to apply national rules for aviation emissions trading comparable to the EU ETS or, more generally, that it will pursue legal dumping in respect of environmental protection. However, there may be some temptation in the UK to aid its air carriers by withdrawing aviation from emissions trading or to facilitate economic development (e.g. the expansion of Heathrow airport) at the expense of other environmental standards.[11] Finally, should the UK be outside the EU ETS, the emissions trading schemes in the UK and EU27 could perhaps be internationally harmonised by voluntary participation in ICAO global Carbon Offsetting and Reduction Scheme for International Aviation (CORSIA).[12]

---

11 However, it is unlikely that the EU would remain passive in the face of the UK's environmental dumping. In particular, the EU may reverse its 'stop-the-clock' decision concerning the EU ETS.

12 For general implications of Brexit for environmental law see eg: I Hadjyianni, 'The UK and the World: Environmental Law' in PJ Birkinshaw and A Biondi (eds), *Britain Alone! The Implications and Consequences of the United Kingdom Exit from the EU* (Wolters Kluwer 2016); E Scotford and M Bowman, 'Brexit and Environmental Law: Challenges and Opportunities' (2016) 27(3) *King's Law Journal* 416.

9 Air navigation

Issues pertaining to air navigation are the key domain of the Chicago Convention and its annexes. Due to European geography, application of these international rules by EU member states resulted in fragmentation of airspace into many relatively small national areas with distinct air navigation service systems, which caused inefficiencies in dealing with the rising air traffic volumes at the EU level. These problems led to comprehensive, direct harmonisation of air navigation matters in the EU within the Single European Sky (SES) initiative. Two packages of legal measures have been adopted in the EU with an aim to enhance safety standards and air traffic efficiency. The first package (SES I) embraced framework regulation 549/2004 creating the Single European Sky,[1] technical regulations on the provision of air navigation services,[2] organisation and use of the airspace[3] and the interoperability of the European air traffic management network[4]

---

1 Regulation (EC) No 549/2004 of the European Parliament and of the Council of 10 March 2004 laying down the framework for the creation of the single European sky [2004] OJ L96/1.
2 Regulation (EC) No 550/2004 of the European Parliament and of the Council of 10 March 2004 on the provision of air navigation services in the single European sky [2004] OJ L96/10.
3 Regulation (EC) No 551/2004 of the European Parliament and of the Council of 10 March 2004 on the organisation and use of the airspace in the single European sky [2004] OJ L96/20.
4 Regulation (EC) No 552/2004 of the European Parliament and of the Council of 10 March 2004 on the interoperability of the European Air Traffic Management network [2004] OJ L96/26, partly repealed and replaced by provisions of regulation (EU) No 2018/1139 of the European Parliament and of the Council of 4 July 2018 on common rules in the field of civil aviation and establishing a European Union Aviation Safety Agency, and amending Regulations (EC) No 2111/2005, (EC) No 1008/2008, (EU) No 996/2010, (EU) No 376/2014 and Directives 2014/30/EU and 2014/53/EU of the European Parliament and of the Council, and repealing Regulations (EC) No 552/2004 and (EC) No 216/2008 of the European Parliament and of the Council and Council Regulation (EEC) No 3922/91 [2018] OJ L 212/1.

and implementing regulations issued by the European Commission. In the second package (SES II), these acts were revised to improve performance of the air traffic management system including regulation 1070/2009[5] and implementing regulations. At the same time, the SES initiative has been firmly linked with the EU aviation safety regulatory framework.[6] By means of regulation 1108/2009,[7] the system built upon regulation 216/2008[8] has been expanded in respect of aerodromes, air traffic management and air navigation services. This has also meant a move of competences concerning rulemaking support and oversight of member states from EUROCONTROL to EASA. This is continued under new framework regulation 2018/1139.

The key idea of the reformed SES consists in distinguishing the European Upper Flight Information Region (EUIR) and its reconfiguration into Functional Air Blocks (FABs). FABs transgress national frontiers and are created based on traffic characteristics in order to optimise operational efficiency of air navigation services (ANS). Nine FABs have been established by agreements between EU, EEA, ECAA member states and Switzerland, and notified to the European Commission. Since ANS are financed through air navigation charges, the SES initiative includes a common ANS charging scheme. A network manager has been established within the SES project to deliver air traffic management (ATM) functions concerning route network design and air traffic flow management. The network manager is also responsible for allocation of frequencies and transponder codes and managing network crisis. Until the end of 2019, this role has been mandated by the European Commission to EUROCONTROL, which also performs ATM functions for its non-EU members and other states. Finally, the technical development of the SES is supported by the Single European Sky ATM Research (SESAR) programme aimed at modernising infrastructure and optimising capacity.

5 Regulation (EC) No 1070/2009 of the European Parliament and of the Council of 21 October 2009 amending Regulations (EC) No 549/2004, (EC) No 550/2004, (EC) No 551/2004 and (EC) No 552/2004 in order to improve the performance and sustainability of the European aviation system [2009] OJ L300/34.

6 See Chapter 6 of this book.

7 Regulation (EC) No 1108/2009 of the European Parliament and of the Council of 21 October 2009 amending Regulation (EC) No 216/2008 in the field of aerodromes, air traffic management and air navigation services and repealing Directive 2006/23/EC [2009] OJ L309/51.

8 Regulation (EC) No 216/2008 of the European Parliament and of the Council of 20 February 2008 on common rules in the field of civil aviation and establishing a European Aviation Safety Agency, and repealing Council Directive 91/670/EEC, Regulation (EC) No 1592/2002 and Directive 2004/36/EC [2008] OJ L79/1, now replaced by regulation 2018/1139.

Brexit will change the functioning of the whole SES framework, to which the UK is an important contributor. First, EU regulations concerning ATM and ANS will stop applying to the UK. This will threaten functioning of the UK-Irish FAB, which was the first one to be established. This block handles 80% of North Atlantic air traffic. National Air Traffic Services (NATS), the British ANS Provider (ANSP) which serves this FAB, is also engaged in the Borealis Free Route Airspace (FRA) project[9] together with other north European ANSPs representing two other FABs. Second, after Brexit, the UK ANSP will not be bound by the EU common ANS charging scheme. However, any post-Brexit UK charging schemes will still have to follow the EUROCONTROL agreement on route charges and respect the non-discrimination principle set up in Article 15 of the Chicago Convention. Third, the UK will remain a member of EUROCONTROL, although it will not be covered by the EU-mandated activity of this organisation. Finally, Brexit will also cut the UK off from the SESAR programme, which will have negative consequences for Britain and the programme itself.

Generally, over the years, the EU air navigation regulation has greatly developed and has gradually led to an important technical rearrangement of European ATM/ANS within a harmonised performance-based system focused on a pan-European air network. Return to pre-SES regulation and ATM/ANS organisation in the UK will lead not only to duplication of effort, but also to the legal and technical fragmentation of the European airspace,[10] which will have adverse long-term implications for network effectiveness, airline costs, punctuality of air services and their environmental footprint. Therefore, it seems that the UK and EU27 will need to find a way to maintain and advance the current SES framework post-Brexit. For instance, EU arrangements with Switzerland and the EEA states may serve as one direction. These countries are involved in the SES initiative. The SES is also designed to progressively expand to ECAA and Euromed partners. The UK's further participation in SESAR will also require an agreement with the EU27 and is likely to be subject to the UK's financial contribution to this programme.

---

9 An FRA is a specified airspace within which users can freely plan a route between a defined entry point and a defined exit point, with the possibility of routing via intermediate (published or unpublished) waypoints, without reference to the air traffic services (ATS) route network, subject of course to availability. See 'Free route airspace (FRA)' (*EUROCONTROL*, date unknown) <www.eurocontrol.int/articles/free-route-airspace> accessed 28 April 2018.

10 L Vrbaski, 'Flying into the Unknown: The UK's Air Transport Relations with the European Union and Third Countries Following "Brexit"' (2016) 41(6) *Air & Space Law* 421, 428–429.

Brexit will also have impact on more general EU transport-related projects that are relevant to air navigation. The Trans-European Networks (TENs) in the area of transport, energy and telecommunications infrastructures are an EU policy outlined in Articles 170–172 TFEU aimed at ensuring accessibility, interconnection and interoperability of national infrastructure networks. One of the TENs is the Trans-European Transport Network (TEN-T). It is defined in regulation 1315/2013[11] and is organised as a Comprehensive Network which encompasses airports and a Core Network consisting of those parts of the comprehensive network which are of the highest strategic importance. The TEN-T infrastructure requirements refer to the implementation of SES and SESAR. After Brexit, the TEN-T networks will need to be reconfigured, which will necessarily involve an amendment to regulation 1315/2013. The EU's global navigation satellite system (GNSS) Galileo programme will also be disturbed by Brexit. In particular, the UK will be deprived of access to the Galileo Public Regulated Service (PRS). Second, with the British aerospace industry being outside the EU, the technical development of this programme will be hindered. Therefore, a UK-EU27 arrangement in this area will be welcome.

11 Regulation (EU) No 1315/2013 of the European Parliament and of the Council of 11 December 2013 on Union guidelines for the development of the trans-European transport network and repealing Decision No 661/2010/EU [2013] OJ L348/1.

10 Aerospace manufacturing

Aerospace manufacturing activity as such is not a distinct subject of EU law. However, this activity is governed by numerous parts of EU law including aviation-specific regulations, which facilitate trans-border aerospace production in the EU. Importantly, the UK represents the largest national aerospace sector in the EU, supporting 120,000 jobs. It generates a yearly revenue of more than GBP 32 billion, of which GBP 28 billion is exported,[1] with GBP 8 billion being exported within the EU.[2] The UK industry will be directly hit by Brexit. Additionally, several continental and British manufacturers have overseas production facilities across the English Channel (e.g. Airbus operates a wings factory in Broughton). The EU aerospace sector is also dependent on intra-community supply of components.[3] The UK's departure from the EU may also jeopardise some defence projects between EU member states.[4] Not surprisingly, aviation stakeholders have been concerned with the impact of Brexit on the British and European aerospace industry.

1 ADS Group, *2017 Industry Facts & Figures. A Guide to the UK's Aerospace, Defence, Security & Space Sectors* (ADS 2017) 8 (data as of 2016).
2 T Osborne, 'Brexit Dilemmas' (2016) 178(14) *Aviation Week & Space Technology* 42. The forerunner of this article appeared online under a different title, but is subscription only: T Osborne, 'Brexit Damage Control Plans for UK Aerospace and Defense' (*Aviation Week*, 1 July 2016) <http://aviationweek.com/defense/brexit-damage-control-plans-uk-aerospace-and-defense> accessed 7 August 2018.
3 See e.g. D Thisdell, 'Brexit casts shadow over UK aerospace' (*FlightGlobal*, 15 June 2017) <www.flightglobal.com/news/articles/analysis-brexit-casts-shadow-over-uk-aerospace-437582/> accessed 13 June 2018.
4 See e.g. B Callan, 'Defense High and Low Roads After Brexit' (2016) 178(14) *Aviation Week & Space Technology*; D Perry, 'Dassault plays down Brexit fears over Anglo-French UCAV project' (*Flightglobal.com*, 10 March 2017) <www.flightglobal.com/news/articles/dassault-plays-down-brexit-fears-over-anglo-french-u-435036/> accessed 13 June 2018.

The primary area of aviation law relevant for the aerospace industry where Brexit will leave an imprint is aviation safety regulations, namely technical requirements for aviation products. On and after Exit Day, the UK will not be bound by the regulation 2018/1139[5] framework and the EASA system and will not benefit from the EU-third party agreements concerning recognition of technical approvals. Unless a UK-EU27 agreement extends the application of the EU aviation safety *acquis* to the UK, the operation of British-based manufacturers will rely on domestic laws. It is, however, uncertain if the UK will manage to substitute the EU regulatory legacy. One thing is certain: any future discrepancies between the British and EU laws will generally be a barrier for the industry.[6]

The two other legal pillars of the EU aerospace sector are the Treaty freedoms concerning movement of goods and people. As mentioned, efficient and timely intra-community supply of components is an important element of the European aerospace industry, which relies on just-in-time processes. This activity is currently secured by the EU customs union.[7] Introduction of any tariffs and customs restrictions will impede import and export of aviation products between the UK and the EU27 and will lead to higher prices in the supply chain.[8] The British industry is also dependent on recruiting skilled aerospace workers on the continent, and this ability will not be protected by the Treaty after Brexit.[9] The future British position in the

5 Regulation (EU) No 2018/1139 of the European Parliament and of the Council of 4 July 2018 on common rules in the field of civil aviation and establishing a European Union Aviation Safety Agency, and amending Regulations (EC) No 2111/2005, (EC) No 1008/2008, (EU) No 996/2010, (EU) No 376/2014 and Directives 2014/30/EU and 2014/53/EU of the European Parliament and of the Council, and repealing Regulations (EC) No 552/2004 and (EC) No 216/2008 of the European Parliament and of the Council and Council Regulation (EEC) No 3922/91 [2018] OJ L 212/1.

6 See also Chapter 6 of this book. However, some point out that escaping EU regulations could inspire innovation and development of the drone sector in the UK, for instance; see T Robinson, 'Tailwind or turbulence? Brexit and UK aerospace' (Royal Aeronautical Society, 6 December 2016) <www.aerosociety.com/news/tailwind-or-turbulence-brexit-and-uk-aerospace/> accessed 13 June 2018.

7 The continued circulation of goods placed on the market shall be secured after Brexit by means of an UK-EU27 arrangement; see Part Three Title I of Draft Withdrawal Agreement of 19 March 2018, TF50 (2018). For transitional provisions for ongoing movement of goods, see Part Three Title II of this draft.

8 See Business, Energy and Industrial Strategy Committee, 'The impact of Brexit on the aerospace sector' (HC 2017–19, HC 380) 7–9.

9 However, the rights of the existing migrant workers (self-employed persons) in the host state and frontier workers (self-employed persons) shall be protected after Brexit by the Withdrawal Agreement. See preliminarily accepted provisions included in Part Two Title II Chapter 2 of Draft Withdrawal Agreement of 19 March 2018, TF50 (2018) 35.

European Space Agency (ESA) and in EU space projects (Galileo, EGNOS, Copernicus)[10] and other aerospace research and development projects, as well as its participation in the European Defence Agency (EDA) projects and programmes,[11] will also be important for the UK aerospace industry. These stated legal characteristics mean that a simple UK-EU27 aviation agreement would be insufficient to protect uninterrupted operations of the aerospace industry. To achieve this goal, the post-Brexit deal would have to harmonise technical standards in the first place. This should be accompanied by regulations enabling trans-border employment. Levying customs duties for aerospace products would also be required, although at least as regards civil aircraft, their engines, subassemblies, parts and components, this effect can be partly achieved by means of the existing WTO agreement on trade in aircraft.[12] UK participation in EU aerospace and defence projects and programmes will require additional agreements.

10 The European Space Agency is based on the Convention for the establishment of a European Space Agency, done in Paris on 30 May 1975, UNTS, Vol 1297, No 21524, entered into force on 30 October 1980. The UK is and will remain a party to this convention and a member of ESA after Brexit. The EU and ESA are linked by means of the Framework Agreement between the European Community and the European Space Agency, signed in Brussels on 25 November 2003 [2004] OJ L261/64, entered into force on 28 May 2004. The ESA and EUROCONTROL are engaged in the Galileo and European Geostationary Navigation Overlay Service (EGNOS) programmes based on the Agreement between the European Community, the European Space Agency and the European Organisation for the Safety of Air Navigation on a European Contribution to the development of a global navigation satellite system (GNSS), signed in Luxembourg on 18 June 1998 [1998] OJ L194/16, entered into force as of the date of signature. Separate agreements have been signed by the EU with the ESA and other agencies as regards the implementation of the Copernicus programme. However, these space programmes themselves are governed by EU law and the exploitation of Galileo and EGNOS is vested in the European GNSS Agency (GSA), which is an EU institution.
11 The EDA is an intergovernmental agency of the Council of the EU, and the UK will not be able to participate in it after Brexit. However, the EDA has signed Administrative Arrangements with several non-EU states (Norway, Switzerland, Serbia and Ukraine), enabling them to participate in its projects and programmes.
12 See also Chapter 1.6 of this book. Note that not all EU member states are parties to this agreement.

11 Aircraft finance

Aircraft finance issues are only fragmentarily governed by EU law. Notwithstanding the basic freedom of movement of capital (Article 63 TFEU), EU law incorporates other regulations that will be relevant to aircraft finance in the context of Brexit. Also, the application of some EU member state laws may change after the UK's departure from the EU.

First, EU law imposes some limitations on aircraft leasing. Article 4(c) of regulation 1008/2008[1] requires that an EU air carrier has at least one aircraft at its disposal through ownership or a dry lease agreement. At the same time, Article 13 of this regulation allows EU airlines to enter into wet lease agreements. According to this Article, wet lease agreements under which the EU air carrier is the lessee and all dry lease agreements are subject to aviation safety approvals. Additionally, wet lease of aircraft registered in a third country by an EU air carrier requires operating approval in the EU. As these provisions will cease to apply to the UK on Exit Day, Britain will be free to regulate these issues on its own. At the same time, the UK will be regarded as a third country for wet lease purposes in EU27 member states.

Second, English law is commonly chosen as the governing law of financing transactions, even if they have no geographic connection with the UK. The substance of this law will, however, not be affected by the UK's departure from the EU. The contractual choice of law will be respected subject to the existing laws, which will not be disturbed by Brexit. Not least, the choice of English law will still be respected in the EU27.[2] Nevertheless,

---

1 Regulation (EC) No 1008/2008 of the European Parliament and of the Council of 24 September 2008 on common rules for the operation of air services in the Community [2008] OJ L293/3.
2 According to regulation (EC) No 593/2008 of the European Parliament and of the Council of 17 June 2008 on the law applicable to contractual obligations (Rome I) [2008] OJ L177/6, contracts shall be governed by the law chosen by the parties whether or not it is the law of an EU member state.

in UK-EU27 relations Brexit may bring about problems concerning jurisdiction and enforceability of judgements, which may complicate aircraft
financing transactions.[3]

Third, Brexit may have an impact on aircraft registration rules. Aircraft ownership is the domain of national laws and is neither governed
by the Chicago Convention nor directly regulated by EU aviation law.
Save for states where aircraft registry is open to foreign operators (open
registries), usually only the national of a state (or the company which is
registered or has a principal place of business there) is qualified to regis-
ter aircraft in that state. Some EU member states' domestic laws extend
these eligibility criteria to nationals (companies) of other EU/EEA member states (e.g. this is the case in the UK[4]). After Brexit, any such laws
in the EU27 member states will not cover UK nationals and companies.
At the same time, the registration eligibility criteria in the UK will not
be automatically changed by Brexit.[5] However, they may be amended by
British lawmakers.

Finally, Brexit may introduce changes as regards laws governing security
agreements, which usually accompany aircraft financing transactions. The
core of financial security law was traditionally a domain of the domestic
regulations of the state in which the aircraft registry was located. These
laws presented different approaches to securities and their international
enforcement was impeded by the fact that aircraft have no fixed location.
To facilitate aircraft financing, the CTC has created an international interest
in aircraft engines and helicopters that is recognised in all of the contracting
states. Both the UK and the EU are parties to the CTC and its aircraft protocol. Brexit itself will not change that.[6] However, Brexit will have an impact
on the application of the CTC system in the UK. First, the CTC-relevant
EU regulations (Rome I regulation,[7] recast Brussels regulation,[8] and insolvency proceedings regulation)[9] will cease to apply in the UK along with
the EU declaration made under Article 55 CTC. These issues will either be

3 These general contract law issues exceed the scope of this book.
4 See Part 3 of the Air Navigation Order 2016, SI 2016/765.
5 Assuming the successful passage of the European Union (Withdrawal) Bill, which will
   provide for the relevant secondary legislation to be 'saved'.
6 See Chapter 1.7 of this book.
7 Regulation (EC) No 593/2008 of the European Parliament and of the Council of
   17 June 2008 on the law applicable to contractual obligations (Rome I) [2008] OJ L177/6.
8 Regulation (EU) No 1215/2012 of the European Parliament and of the Council of 12
   December 2012 on jurisdiction and the recognition and enforcement of judgments in civil
   and commercial matters [2012] OJ L351/1.
9 Regulation (EU) 2015/848 of the European Parliament and of the Council of 20 May 2015
   on insolvency proceedings [2015] OJ L141/19.

arranged between the UK and the EU27[10] or will be entirely subject to existing or to new British laws. Under these circumstances, London will need to consider replacement or amendment of its laws implementing the CTC in the first place,[11] as well as lodging new declarations under the CTC and the protocol as to any issues previously within EU competence.

10 According to Article 62 of Draft Withdrawal Agreement of 19 March 2018, TF50 (2018) 35, the UK has preliminarily agreed to be bound by the Rome I regulation in respect of contracts concluded before the end of the transition period. There is also preliminary agreement as to transitional provisions as to the application of the recast Brussels regulation and the insolvency proceedings regulation (Article 63 of Draft Withdrawal Agreement), see 'Joint statement from the negotiators of the European Union and the United Kingdom Government on progress of negotiations under Article 50 TEU on the United Kingdom's orderly withdrawal from the European Union', 19 June 2018, TF50 (2018) 52.
11 See L Vrbaski, 'Flying into the Unknown: The UK's Air Transport Relations with the European Union and Third Countries Following "Brexit"' (2016) 41(6) *Air & Space Law* 421, 432.

12   Civil liability

Brexit will have impact on the current air carrier liability laws applicable in the UK. First, unless otherwise arranged, regulation 261/2004[1] will not apply to and in the UK after its exit from the EU. This regulation defines air passenger rights in case of denied boarding, flight cancellation and delay or downgrading. Subject to circumstances, passengers shall be offered accommodation, rerouting and access to refreshments at the expense of the operating carrier. They are also entitled to claim a fixed compensation, which does not exclude further compensation claims. The scope of application of regulation 261/2004 is key to understanding the impact of Brexit on passenger rights. The regulation applies to passengers departing from an airport located in the territory of a member state. This concerns all intra-EU operations, including domestic flights in the territories of EU member states as well as flights to an airport located in a third country, irrespective of the nationality of the operating carrier. Flights from an airport located in a third country to the EU are also governed by the regulation, however, only if they are operated by an EU air carrier.

Accordingly, Brexit will have impact on flights in various ways. Regulation 261/2004 will not apply to the UK; however, it will be directly incorporated into the British legal system by means of the European Union (Withdrawal) Act 2018.[2] Even so, its actual application in the UK will rely on the future adaptations of the regulation that will be necessary. The UK may also decide to abandon this regulation. This may lead to some deregulation, in particular as regards flights between the UK and third countries, and British domestic flights. From the EU27 perspective, provisions of the regulation will remain

---

1 Regulation (EC) No 261/2004 of the European Parliament and of the Council of 11 February 2004 establishing common rules on compensation and assistance to passengers in the event of denied boarding and of cancellation or long delay of flights, and repealing Regulation (EEC) No 295/91 [2004] OJ L46/1.
2 European Union (Withdrawal) Act 2018, 2018 ch 16. See Chapter 18 of this book.

unchanged; however, in UK-EU27 relations, they will apply to all EU27 air carriers' operations and only to those UK airlines' operations which depart from airports in EU27 member states.[3] In any case, the outcome of Brexit in respect of regulation 261/2004 would be beneficial for UK airlines, but not for passengers, who could be deprived of existing protection. Total deregulation in UK-third party relations could possibly also move some intercontinental air traffic operated by third-party carriers from the EU27 airports to British airports. However, it is questionable if the UK will be able to take full advantage of this situation and become a 261-free European hub. Such a policy would require wide access to the EU27 feeding market, whereas the EU27 will likely make any open skies deal conditional upon the acceptance by the UK of rules encompassed in regulation 261/2004.[4]

The Warsaw-Montreal system contains liability rules for international carriage by air. This includes limits of air carrier liability in case of death or injury of passengers, and in relation to delay, baggage and cargo. The provisions of the Warsaw Convention, as amended, and the Montreal Convention will remain binding in the UK after Brexit. However, the EU, which is party to the Montreal Convention, has adopted some regulations which implement or supplement its provisions. In particular, regulation (EC) No 889/2002[5] expands the application of Montreal Convention provisions to air carriage within a single EU member state. In respect of passengers and their baggage (not cargo), this regulation explicitly submits all EU air carriers to the relevant liability rules established in the Montreal Convention. Additionally, regulation 785/2004[6] sets out minimum insurance requirements in respect of passengers, baggage, cargo and third parties for all air carriers and to all aircraft operators flying within, into, out of, or over the territory of a member state.[7]

3 Flights operated by UK air carriers from the UK to EU27 member states will be outside the scope of the regulation, since these carriers will no longer qualify as EU air carriers. Note that this holds true even if the UK applies the regulation unilaterally. The only way to preserve the current scope of application of regulation 261/2004 in UK-EU27 relations is through a UK-EU27 aviation arrangement.

4 L Vrbaski, 'Flying into the Unknown: The UK's Air Transport Relations with the European Union and Third Countries Following "Brexit" ' (2016) 41(6) *Air & Space Law* 421, 433.

5 Regulation (EC) No 889/2002 of the European Parliament and of the Council of 13 May 2002 amending Council Regulation (EC) No 2027/97 on air carrier liability in the event of accidents [2002] OJ L140/2.

6 Regulation (EC) No 785/2004 of the European Parliament and of the Council of 21 April 2004 on insurance requirements for air carriers and aircraft operators [2004] OJ L138/1.

7 This is supplemented by Article 11 of regulation (EC) No 1008/2008 of the European Parliament and of the Council of 24 September 2008 on common rules for the operation of air services in the Community [2008] OJ L293/3 which requires air carriers to be insured to cover liability in case of accidents with respect to mail. The Montreal Convention does not encompass specific liability rules in respect of postal items.

Brexit will have no influence on any rights and obligations arising straight from the Montreal Convention. However, if the UK so decides, the regulations which implement or supplement provisions of the convention may not apply in the UK after its withdrawal from the EU.[8] In such case, the first consequence will be that international carriage by air between the UK and aviation partners including EU27 member states will be regulated directly by the Warsaw Convention or Montreal Convention, depending on the status of the partners to these conventions.[9] Second, carriage by air within the UK will be subject only to British law, which will not necessarily need to adhere to the Montreal Convention standards after Brexit. Finally, the insurance requirements for UK air carriers will be governed by British law,[10] although UK air carriers flying into, out of, or over the territory of an EU27 member state will still be subjected to regulation 785/2004.

8 EU regulations will be incorporated into the British legal system by the European Union (Withdrawal) Act 2018, although they may be deregulated for the air carriers' benefit, just as in case of regulation 261/2004.
9 Note that all EU27 member states are parties to the Montreal Convention.
10 According to Article 50 of the Montreal Convention states parties shall require their carriers to maintain adequate insurance covering their liability under the convention.

13 Aircrew rights

The freedom of movement for workers (Article 45 TFEU) and the harmonisation of qualifications of flying personnel within the regulation 2018/1139[1] framework,[2] has enabled trans-border employment of aircrews in the EU. Such practice raises trans-border issues in relation to aircrew rights. Social security matters have been generally coordinated by regulation 883/2004.[3] Under this law, a person employed as aircrew can only be protected by social security legislation of the member state in which the person has their home base (i.e. the place where the person's actual work begins and ends). Labour rights are generally a matter of member states' domestic laws, although some minimum standards are imposed by EU directives. That notwithstanding, and irrespective of the form of employment and of the law governing an employment contract, for safety reasons, aircrews' flight and duty times are directly harmonised at the EU level.[4]

1 Regulation (EU) No 2018/1139 of the European Parliament and of the Council of 4 July 2018 on common rules in the field of civil aviation and establishing a European Union Aviation Safety Agency, and amending Regulations (EC) No 2111/2005, (EC) No 1008/2008, (EU) No 996/2010, (EU) No 376/2014 and Directives 2014/30/EU and 2014/53/EU of the European Parliament and of the Council, and repealing Regulations (EC) No 552/2004 and (EC) No 216/2008 of the European Parliament and of the Council and Council Regulation (EEC) No 3922/91 [2018] OJ L 212/1.

2 See Commission Regulation (EU) No 1178/2011 of 3 November 2011 laying down technical requirements and administrative procedures related to civil aviation aircrew pursuant to Regulation (EC) No 216/2008 of the European Parliament and of the Council [2011] OJ L311/1. See also Chapter 6 of this book.

3 Regulation (EC) No 883/2004 of the European Parliament and of the Council of 29 April 2004 on the coordination of social security systems [2004] OJ L166/1.

4 Commission Regulation (EU) No 83/2014 of 29 January 2014 amending Regulation (EU) No 965/2012 laying down technical requirements and administrative procedures related to air operations pursuant to Regulation (EC) No 216/2008 of the European Parliament and of the Council [2014] OJ L28/17.

The described system supports the mobility of the European workforce in aviation, and shields basic labour rights. To some extent, it also enables EU airlines to choose between different jurisdictions when employing aircrews in order to avoid the more burdensome national regimes. It also allows EU air carriers to bring their employees to other EU member states for the purpose of operating services there. When the UK leaves the EU, these rules will cease to apply to and in the UK, and to UK-EU27 relations. The employment of aircrews originating from EU27 member states in the UK and *vice versa* will be subject to domestic laws of the UK and EU27 member states,[5] respectively.[6] In the usual course of events, the practice of bringing personnel to the territory of the other party, and of maintaining them in that territory, will rely on the provisions of revived UK-EU27 bilateral air services agreements. On and after Exit Day, aircrews' flight and duty times in the UK will be governed directly by British law.[7] The same will apply to licensing of flying personnel and recognition of qualifications.[8]

5 EU law does not govern employment in relation to third-country nationals working on board aircraft.
6 As to the rights of the existing migrant workers (self-employed persons) in the host state and frontier workers (self-employed persons), see preliminarily accepted provisions included in Part Two Title II Chapter 2 of Draft Withdrawal Agreement of 19 March 2018, TF50 (2018) 35. As to post-Brexit social security rights concerning such persons, see preliminarily accepted provisions included in Part Two Title III of this draft.
7 Existence of such domestic rules is obligatory subject to ICAO standards for Crew Fatigue Management established in Annex 6 to the Chicago Convention.
8 Save for possible opt-outs, the licensing provisions shall conform with ICAO standards contained in Annex 1 to the Chicago Convention.

Part III

Impact on institutions and proceedings

The previous part has indicated which groups of legal acts will be affected or left intact by Brexit. In particular, many legal acts will cease applying to the UK, and to UK-EU27 traffic. These areas will either be governed by the Brexit-resistant legal acts or British laws, or will lack any regulation whatsoever. In such cases, the emergent legal gaps will need to be filled by British and international lawmakers, a process which will also involve UK-EU27 aviation arrangements.

The aim of this part is to show the impact of the Brexit-transformed legal environment on particular aviation activities. It will be explained how legal changes will translate into practical problems in the industry. Just as in the previous part, in the first place a hard-Brexit scenario will be considered whereby no deal is reached between the UK and the EU27 or between the UK and third parties as to the matters under discussion (not that there is no deal at all). It will be indicated which of the relevant aviation regulations will stop applying and which of them will stay in place. Where relevant, the role of British legislation preserving EU laws domestically and the recommendations for post-Brexit solutions will be outlined, whereas a possible transition period when current aviation laws could be applied *mutatis mutandis* in or to the UK will generally be left aside.[1]

---

1 These issues will be discussed in detail in Part IV of this book. Where special provisions for the transition period or for continued application of EU law have already been proposed in EU-UK negotiations as of 19 June 2018, this will also be mentioned in footnotes in the present part of the book.

14 Legislative branch

The impact of Brexit on the distribution of legislative powers will be quite straightforward. Within the scope of EU competences, these powers are normally realised by the European Parliament and the Council. They may also be exercised by the European Commission, should the Treaties so provide. The powers conferred on EU institutions will not cover the UK after Brexit. Hence, all law-making matters currently dealt with by those institutions will become the domain of the British legislature, primarily the UK Parliament,[1] although depending on the subject of the legislation, some matters may be passed by the UK Parliament to the executive.[2] The transfer of powers from the EU to the UK does not necessarily mean that the British legislature must undertake the challenge of regulating all issues previously reigned over by EU law. However, due to the scope of post-Brexit legal gaps, this will usually be the case. Given the extent of EU aviation regulations, it will be extremely difficult for the UK to rebuild aviation legislation, in particular given that in its regulatory activity the UK will not be assisted by EU bodies.

As regards pending legislative business, Brexit will bring mixed results. The UK will obviously not be bound by any EU laws that will enter into force on Exit Day or after.[3] EU acts which enter into force before that day will apply in the UK until Brexit. EU laws issued before Exit Day but entering into force on that day or after will not be binding upon the UK. Any EU-derived laws which enter into force before Exit Day and which require

---

1 It seems there will not be much involvement for the devolved legislatures, since key parts of civil aviation regulation in the UK are the exclusive competence of the Westminster Parliament.
2 For the planned scope of delegated powers, see also Chapter 18 of this book.
3 However, a transition period has been proposed. During that period, EU law would apply to and in the UK. See Chapter 17 of this book.

implementation in member states' legal orders, according to Article 291(1) TFEU, shall be duly implemented by the UK, and will be 'saved' by operation of the European Union (Withdrawal) Act 2018,[4] even though they may be repealed thereafter. However, this obligation shall not concern directives with post-Brexit transposition dates. Finally, notwithstanding implementation of EU derived law, any UK laws which enter into force before Brexit will need to respect limitations arising directly from the Treaties (e.g. Treaty freedoms).

The UK's exit from the EU will not directly impact upon EU legislative procedures. The relevant provisions of the Treaties will be left intact by Brexit, but without Britain the arithmetic of voting in the EU will change. This will first and foremost concern voting in the Council, which consists of representatives of member states. Except where the Treaties provide otherwise, the Council acts by a qualified majority defined as at least 55% of the members of the Council, comprising at least 15 of them and representing member states comprising at least 65% of the population of the EU (Article 16[4] TEU). Within the EU, Britain has regularly been a strong supporter of liberalisation initiatives concerning aviation. Therefore, some worries have been expressed that without the UK's voice, EU aviation policies and regulations may become more restrictive.[5]

---

4 European Union (Withdrawal) Act 2018, 2018 ch 16.
5 Centre for Asia Pacific Aviation, 'Brexit and aviation Part 1: Open Pandora's box and anything can happen. But status quo is likely' (*CAPA News*, 27 June 2016) <https://cen treforaviation.com/insights/analysis/brexit-and-aviation-part-1-open-pandoras-box-and-anything-can-happen-but-status-quo-is-likely-288477> accessed 13 June 2018.

15 Executive branch

After Brexit, the executive powers vested in the EU institutions will have to be taken over by respective British authorities.[1] As regards civil aviation, executive powers in the EU are generally exercised by the European Commission and, under the framework of regulation 2018/1139, also by the EASA.[2] The basic powers in all areas of EU competences in aviation are concentrated in the European Commission. These powers include, but are not limited to, conducting administrative proceedings and issuing administrative decisions. In particular, the European Commission is competent to review or approve some decisions of the member states' authorities or to review member states' compliance with EU aviation laws. With respect to these investigations, the Commission can make its own decisions.[3] It can also request some administrative actions from the member states,[4] designate other entities to carry out some administrative tasks governed by EU aviation law[5] and publish notices in the *Official Journal of the European*

---

1 However, a transition period has been proposed; see Chapter 17 of this book.
2 Regulation (EU) No 2018/1139 of the European Parliament and of the Council of 4 July 2018 on common rules in the field of civil aviation and establishing a European Union Aviation Safety Agency, and amending Regulations (EC) No 2111/2005, (EC) No 1008/2008, (EU) No 996/2010, (EU) No 376/2014 and Directives 2014/30/EU and 2014/53/EU of the European Parliament and of the Council, and repealing Regulations (EC) No 552/2004 and (EC) No 216/2008 of the European Parliament and of the Council and Council Regulation (EEC) No 3922/91 [2018] OJ L 212/1.
3 See, e.g. Article 16 of regulation (EC) No 550/2004 of the European Parliament and of the Council of 10 March 2004 on the provision of air navigation services in the single European sky, [2004] OJ L96/10; Articles 67(2–3) and 71(2) of regulation 2018/1139; Articles 15(3) and 18(2) of regulation (EC) No 1008/2008 of the European Parliament and of the Council of 24 September 2008 on common rules for the operation of air services in the Community [2008] OJ L293/3.
4 See, e.g. Article 8(2)(c) of regulation 1008/2008.
5 See, e.g. Article 11(2) of regulation (EC) No 549/2004 of the European Parliament and of the Council of 10 March 2004 laying down the framework for the creation of the single European sky, [2004] OJ L96/1; Article 9b(1) of regulation 550/2004.

Union.[6] The Commission's competences are correlated with member states' rights and obligations. For instance, member states are required to transfer certain information to the Commission.[7] They are also entitled to request reviews by the Commission.[8]

After Brexit, the Commission's executive powers will not impact upon the UK. Accordingly, all of the UK's corollary rights and obligations will expire. Some of the Commission's competences will have to be taken over by British authorities. However, in many cases, these powers are unique to the EU legal system and it will not be necessary to re-establish them at UK level. Brexit will also not need to involve any transfer of powers as regards those parts of EU law for which execution is already entrusted to member states (e.g. economic regulation). In such cases, only the substantive laws will have to be re-enacted in the UK.

It will be otherwise with regard to aviation safety issues where not only has substantive law been directly harmonised in the EU but also its implementation and execution has been largely concentrated at the community level and vested in the EASA. This agency carries out, on behalf of EU member states, some functions and tasks ascribed to it by applicable international law, namely the Chicago Convention. In its fields of competence, the EASA conducts inspections and investigations and takes necessary measures within the powers conferred on it by regulation 2018/1139 or other EU legislation. In particular, where regulation 2018/1139 is concerned, the EASA is empowered to take decisions for the application of Article 77 (airworthiness and environmental certification with regard to products, parts, non-installed equipment and equipment to control unmanned aircraft remotely), Article 78 (certification of pilot training organisations, cabin crew training organisations, aero-medical centres and flight simulation training devices located outside the territory of the member states), Article 79 (certification of safety-related aerodrome equipment), Article 80 (certification of ATM/ANS organisations located outside the EU, pan-European ATM/ANS organisations and organisations involved in the design, production or maintenance of ATM/ANS systems and ATM/ANS constituents), Article 81 (certification of air traffic controller training organisations located outside the territory of the member states), and Article 82 (authorisation of third-country operators performing commercial air transport operations into the EU). The EASA is also empowered to conduct investigations necessary for the performance of its above tasks related to certification, oversight and

---

6 See, e.g. Article 9a(7) of regulation 550/2004; Articles 16(4) and 17(4) of regulation 1008/2008.

7 See, e.g. Articles 4(5) and 8(6) of regulation 550/2004; Article 10(2) of regulation 1008/2008.

8 See, e.g. Article 18(2) of regulation 1008/2008.

enforcement (Article 83), as well as inspections and other monitoring activities aim to ensure the uniform application of this regulation 2018/1139 across the member states.

After Brexit, many of these powers will have to be taken over by the UK Civil Aviation Authority (CAA). This will particularly be the case for any tasks arising from the Chicago Convention carried out by the EASA on behalf of the UK, including certification of aviation products, and will constitute a huge increase in regulatory burden for the UK. It will be extremely difficult, if possible at all, for the CAA to efficiently re-establish competences in these areas, and it will require vast financial and, above all, human resources. The UK may lack some of these resources, especially given that a large quantity of qualified staff was transferred to the EASA a long time ago. According to some commentators it would even take the UK ten years to re-create an aviation safety administration.[9] The UK's exit from the EASA would also be harmful to the agency itself. The UK is a very significant contributor to the EASA in terms of financing (through the EU budget and through industry participants) and leadership on ideas and policies.[10] It is said that the UK and France supply two-thirds of all the rulemaking input on EU safety regulation, and together undertake close to 90% of EASA's outsourced activities.[11]

Therefore, it would be beneficial for the UK and the EU27 if Britain remained an EASA member.[12] The EASA is an EU agency, although this does not preclude participation of European third states, provided that they are parties to the Chicago Convention. However, according to Article 129 of regulation 2018/1139, third states may only participate in the EASA if they enter into an agreement with the EU for the adoption and application of the EU aviation safety *acquis*. Such agreement defines the rules for the third state's participation in the work of the agency, financial contributions and staff. The status of third states in the EASA is adequate to their level of cooperation with the EU. For instance, EEA states and Switzerland are EASA member states and sit on the agency's Management Board, though

---

9 B Humphreys, 'Brexit and Aviation: All Clear Now?'(2016) XV(3) *Aviation & Space Journal* 30, 40.

10 Centre for Asia Pacific Aviation, 'The great Brexit aviation debate. A transition deal is needed to avoid disaster for UK airlines' (*CAPA News*, 1 November 2017) <https://cen treforaviation.com/insights/analysis/the-great-brexit-aviation-debate-a-transition-deal-is-needed-to-avoid-disaster-for-uk-airlines-380522> accessed 13 June 2018.

11 A Haines, 'The future of open skies post-Brexit' (GAD speech, Civil Aviation Authority, 1 December 2016).

12 Especially given that, with the dissolution of the Joint Aviation Authorities (JAA), there is no other institution to secure harmonization of aviation safety rules in Europe. In 2009, the EASA absorbed most JAA tasks.

without voting rights,[13] the ECAA states have the status of Management Board Observers with an option to become full members, whereas other partners have Working Arrangements over specific issues. Hence, the way for the UK's post-Brexit participation in EASA is open. However, irrespective of the UK-EU27 arrangements, it seems that the UK will not be able to protect continued voting rights on the EASA's Management Board.[14]

Brexit will also disturb ongoing administrative business. Without special interim provisions, proceedings in the UK which are based on EU aviation law (e.g. air carrier certification) would be discontinued when this law stops applying in the UK on Exit Day. To prevent this, transitional procedural rules have been laid down in the European Union (Withdrawal) Act 2018.[15] Proceedings conducted at the EU level by the Commission or the EASA shall also be discontinued when these institutions lose their power to decide on UK-related matters (e.g. certification of British aviation products) and no new UK-related proceedings will be able to be initiated.[16] Proceedings run by EU27 member states' authorities will be unaffected, though only from a procedural perspective.[17]

Any pre-Brexit administrative resolutions taken by British authorities based on EU laws shall automatically become invalid when these laws stop applying in the UK. For this occasion, transitional provisions have been introduced in the European Union (Withdrawal) Act 2018 (Schedule 8 Parts 3 and 4), to ensure that such resolutions are grandfathered in the UK. The post-Brexit status of decisions taken by EU authorities will be more complicated. Unless otherwise arranged, decisions addressed directly to the UK will not bind the UK after its withdrawal from the EU.[18] The outcome of

---

13 See: Paragraph 3(d) of the annex to the decision No 1/2017 of the Joint Community/Switzerland Air Transport Committee set up under the Agreement between the European Community and the Swiss Confederation on Air Transport of 29 November 2017 replacing the Annex to the Agreement between the European Community and the Swiss Confederation on Air Transport (2017/2465/EU) [2017] OJ L348/46; Paragraph 3(q) of the annex to the Decision of the EEA Joint Committee No 163/2011 of 19 December 2011 amending Annex XIII (Transport) to the EEA Agreement.

14 See Article 99(4) of regulation 2018/1139.

15 See also Chapter 18 of this book.

16 However, see EU proposal for transitional provisions included in Articles 88–90 of Draft Withdrawal Agreement of 19 March 2018, TF50 (2018) 35.

17 As already mentioned, any references to EU member states in substantive laws will cease to apply to the UK.

18 However, under Section 3(2) of the European Union (Withdrawal) Act 2018, those EU decisions which form part of direct EU legislation as defined in this statute will be incorporated into UK law after Brexit. Such decisions are indeed legal acts of the EU, not resolutions adopted in administrative procedures.

Brexit is less clear as regards other EU decisions including 'British elements' (e.g. airworthiness certificates of British aviation products). It is likely that some of these decisions will still be considered valid, at least in the EU27.[19] Finally, Brexit will undermine some decisions issued by EU27 member states' authorities under EU aviation law. For instance, Article 8(1) of regulation 1008/2008 declares that an operating licence of an EU air carrier shall be valid as long as the carrier complies with the requirements set forth in this regulation, which contain *inter alia* the EU majority ownership and effective control conditions that may not be met by some airlines after Brexit.[20]

---

19 Such decisions shall also remain valid in the UK subject to grandfather provisions, see Schedule 8 Parts 3 and 4 of the European Union (Withdrawal) Act 2018. This issue could also be resolved in a UK-EU27 arrangement, see EU proposal for the continued legal force and enforceability of EU decisions included in Article 91 of the Draft Withdrawal Agreement of 19 March 2018, TF50 (2018) 35.
20 See also Chapter 3.2 of this book.

16 Judicial branch

The UK exit from the EU will bring about important changes for the judicial branch of the UK and the EU27; however, none of the changes are aviation-specific. Therefore, only key issues will be outlined here. The main result would be that the CJEU will lose its jurisdiction over the UK in respect to all issues dealt with by this court in accordance with the TFEU. Consequently, the UK will lose corresponding rights and obligations defined in the Treaty, including the right to intervene or submit observations in CJEU proceedings.[1] It seems that CJEU proceedings involving the UK shall be discontinued, and no new UK-related cases be brought.[2] Furthermore, after the UK ceases to be a contracting party to the TFEU, Article 280 of this Treaty will no longer secure enforceability of CJEU judgements in the UK.[3] Brexit may also have an effect on pending UK court proceedings pertaining to matters governed by EU law. However, the exact impact on these proceedings will likely depend on their nature and subject. These issues will also be subject to transitional and grandfather provisions introduced by British lawmakers.[4]

Other aspects of court proceedings will also be relevant. As already mentioned, the recast Brussels regulation will cease to apply to the UK, which will have consequences for civil and commercial matters.[5] First, absent this

---

1 However, see EU proposal for the transition period included in Article 86 of Draft Withdrawal Agreement of 19 March 2018, TF50 (2018) 35.
2 A transition period may apply. See EU proposals included in Articles 82–84 of Draft Withdrawal Agreement of 19 March 2018, TF50 (2018) 35.
3 However, see EU proposal for continued binding force and enforcement included in Article 85 of Draft Withdrawal Agreement of 19 March 2018, TF50 (2018) 35.
4 See Schedule 8 Parts 3 and 4 of the European Union (Withdrawal) Act 2018, 2018 ch 16.
5 However, as already mentioned, transitional application of this regulation has preliminarily been agreed (Article 63 of Draft Withdrawal Agreement), see 'Joint statement from the negotiators of the European Union and the United Kingdom Government on progress of negotiations under Article 50 TEU on the United Kingdom's orderly withdrawal from the European Union', 19 June 2018, TF50 (2018) 52.

regulation, UK civil jurisdiction will be defined by British law or international conventions (e.g. the Warsaw Convention or the Montreal Convention). Second, under the recast Brussels regulation, a judgment given in an EU member state is recognised in the other member states without any special procedure being required. It is also enforceable in the other member states without any separate declaration of enforceability. After Brexit, this system will stop working with regard to the UK. Nothing prevents the UK from unilateral transposition of this regulation to its legal order. However, for mutual recognition and enforcement of judgements, an international arrangement between the UK and EU27 member states would still be necessary.

Withdrawal from the EU also means that British courts would no longer be obliged to construe national laws in line with the spirit of the relevant EU rules (consistent interpretation doctrine). Additionally, when freed from the CJEU's legacy, British courts could deliver interpretations of retained EU laws that would depart far from the EU case law. To solve these problems, Sections 5–6 of the European Union (Withdrawal) Act 2018 offer rules as to post-Brexit application of the principle of the supremacy of EU law and interpretation of retained EU law.[6]

6 See also Chapter 18 of this book.

Part IV

Post-Brexit solutions

The previous chapters have presented a hard Brexit scenario whereby the Treaties terminate their effect as to the UK and no legal measures are taken by the UK and the EU27. Part I of the book revealed which legal acts will cease to apply to and in the UK and in the UK's relations with EU27 member states and third parties or will be otherwise affected by Brexit. It also pointed to parts of law that will survive Brexit. The corresponding regulatory problems concerning various aspects of aviation activities have been sketched in Part II.

These discussions show a dramatic picture of a fragmented legal environment characterised by vast legal gaps: an environment that would be totally unworkable for the British aviation industry, and at least inconvenient for EU27 aviation. Preceding chapters have indicated some areas which need to be addressed by the lawmakers post-Brexit. These solutions will be revisited below in a systematic manner. The following part will reveal the level (UK-EU27, UK domestic, UK-third party) at which specific problems should be or have already been addressed, and will examine the possible scope of future arrangements.[1]

Any proposals ahead will be enunciated with the aim to assure uninterrupted post-Brexit activity of the entire European aviation sector to the greatest extent possible. Where the differing interests emergent in some parts of this industry may call for a different policy this will be mentioned. Political obstacles to some types of post-Brexit deals will be mentioned, too.

---

1 The withdrawal of the UK from the EU will also imply some minor legal changes in the EU27 forum. Some provisions of the treaties will need to be changed to reflect Brexit, e.g. Article 52 TEU, Article 355 TFEU and other provisions relating directly to the UK. The agreement on a future relationship between the EU and the UK may possibly also require some adaptations of the Treaties.

17 UK-EU27 forum

The previous chapters show that most post-Brexit problems will arise in UK-EU27 relations. What is more, this is the only forum where the existing legal framework, namely Article 50 TEU, outlines possible post-Brexit solutions and where extensive official guidance material has been published.[1] In this context, it must be acknowledged that Article 50(2) suggests a phased approach to the exit procedure. It states that in the light of the European Council guidelines, the EU shall negotiate and conclude with the exiting state an agreement setting out the arrangements for its withdrawal, taking account of the framework for its future relationship with the EU. This is further elaborated in the Brexit guidelines issued under Article 50(2), which explain that the main objective of the agreement mentioned in Article 50(2) is to ensure an orderly withdrawal from the EU. The Withdrawal Agreement is not meant to constitute a comprehensive post-exit deal that would embrace aviation and other sector-specific matters. The guidelines specify that such deal will be the subject of a separate agreement on a future relationship between the EU and the UK that can only be finalised and concluded once the UK has become a third country. However, Article 50(2) specifies that the Withdrawal Agreement shall take account of the framework for such future arrangement.

---

1 See in particular: European Council, 'Guidelines following the United Kingdom's Notification under Article 50 TEU' (EUCO XT 20004/17, 29 April 2017); European Council, 'European Council (Art. 50) meeting (15 December 2017) – Guidelines' (EUCO XT 20011/17, 15 December 2017); European Council, 'European Council (Art. 50) (23 March 2018) – Guidelines' (EUCO XT 20001/18, 23 March 2018); Council of the EU, 'Directives for the negotiation of an agreement with the United Kingdom of Great Britain and Northern Ireland setting out the arrangements for its withdrawal from the European Union' (XT 21016/17, ADD 1 REV 2, 22 May 2017); Council of the EU, 'Supplementary directives for the negotiation of an agreement with the United Kingdom of Great Britain and Northern Ireland setting out the arrangements for its withdrawal from the European Union' (XT 21004/18, ADD 1 REV 2, 29 January 2018); HM Government, *The United Kingdom's exit from and new partnership with the European Union* (Cm 9417, 2017).

Consequently, the Brexit guidelines envisage two phases of negotiations. In line with Article 50 TEU, the Withdrawal Agreement shall be negotiated in accordance with Article 218(3) TFEU (normally used for EU-third party agreements) and shall be concluded on behalf of the EU by the Council, acting by a qualified majority as defined in Article 238(3)(b) TFEU, after obtaining the consent of the European Parliament.[2] The negotiations with the UK formally commenced on 22 May 2017 and are run on behalf of the EU by the European Commission.[3]

As of 19 June 2018, several issues of a general character have already been preliminarily settled between the UK and the EU.[4] Some of these matters are also relevant to the aviation problems discussed previously. It is worth summarising them. The key conclusion is that the Withdrawal Agreement is planned to enter into force on 30 March 2019, which implies that the UK will not be a member of the EU on that day (Exit Day). This means that the negotiators have not decided to postpone Exit Day by prolonging the application of the treaties to the UK as envisaged in Article 50(3) TEU.[5] However, in line with British requests, they have foreseen transitional application of EU law[6] to and in the UK as a third party until 31 December 2020. The anticipated general rules on transition involve several limitations, with the most important being the exclusion of the UK from participation in EU

---

2 However, the member of the Council representing the withdrawing member state shall not participate in the discussions of the European Council or Council or in decisions concerning it. See Article 50(4) TEU.

3 Council Decision of 22 May 2017 authorising the opening of negotiations with the United Kingdom of Great Britain and Northern Ireland for an agreement setting out the arrangements for its withdrawal from the European Union.

4 See: Draft Withdrawal Agreement of 19 March 2018, TF50 (2018) 35; 'Joint statement from the negotiators of the European Union and the United Kingdom Government on progress of negotiations under Article 50 TEU on the United Kingdom's orderly withdrawal from the European Union', 19 June 2018, TF50 (2018) 52. The progress of Brexit negotiations can be tracked at the following European Commission website: Commission, 'Negotiating documents on Article 50 negotiations with the United Kingdom' (*Europa*, most recently updated 19 June 2018) <https://ec.europa.eu/commission/brexit-negotiations/negotiating-documents-article-50-negotiations-united-kingdom_en> accessed 8 July 2018.

5 According to this provision, absent a Withdrawal Agreement, the UK will leave the EU two years after its notification under Article 50(2) TEU, which means midnight on 29 March 2019 (Brussels time).

6 Which is meant to include: the Treaties, general principles, derived law, international agreements to which the EU is party and the international agreements concluded by the member states acting on behalf of the EU, agreements between member states entered into in their capacity as member states of the EU, acts of the representatives of the governments of the member states meeting within the European Council or the Council of the European Union, and declarations made in the context of intergovernmental conferences which adopted the Treaties.

institutions, offices and agencies, as well as from nomination or election of members to these institutions. The transitional application of EU law is also subject to specific provisions for the transition period proposed in the Draft Withdrawal Agreement. Apart from transition rules, this draft also offers some provisions for the continued post-Brexit application of EU law.[7]

If concluded in line with the current draft, the Withdrawal Agreement will secure, with the aforementioned reservations, the transitional application of the EU aviation *acquis* and other aviation-relevant EU laws in and to the UK until the end of 2020. This will go a long way to provisionally solving the problems in post-Brexit UK-EU27 relations discussed earlier, although not necessarily in UK-third party relations.[8] However, the negotiations of the draft agreement have not been finalised yet, and as emphasised in the EU guidelines, nothing is agreed until everything is agreed.[9]

More interesting from the aviation point of view is the agreement on a future relationship between the EU27 and the UK which may cover specific regulatory issues. The proposal for a transition period has cooled down tempers in the industry, although this solution is still pending final approval. However, even the 31 December 2020 deadline does not seem distant given that the second phase of Brexit negotiations is still at its outset. Only recently has the European Council issued additional guidelines concerning the future scope of the agreement on a future relationship.[10] Airlines usually require 12 months' advance schedule planning, which would suggest that the deal shall be achieved by the end of 2019. This goal is ambitious, assuming that the aviation arrangement will be a part of a wider trade deal. Some time ago, several airlines not surprisingly started introducing clauses to disclaim themselves from the consequences of possible post-Brexit service suspension.[11] Some commentators have drawn attention to the fact that negotiations of other comprehensive international trade agreements have taken 5–10 years.[12] However, the extraordinary 2020 deadline may be ener-

---

7 These issues are not aviation-specific. However, where relevant, the proposed specific transitional provisions and provisions for the continued application of EU law were mentioned in footnotes to the preceding chapters of this book.
8 See Chapter 19 of this book.
9 See: European Council, 'Guidelines following the United Kingdom's Notification under Article 50 TEU' (EUCO XT 20004/17, 29 April 2017) 4; European Council, 'European Council (Art. 50) (23 March 2018) – Guidelines' (EUCO XT 20001/18, 23 March 2018) 1.
10 See European Council, 'European Council (Art. 50) (23 March 2018) – Guidelines' (EUCO XT 20001/18, 23 March 2018).
11 An analogous clause has been proposed for aviation insurance contracts; see L Mueller, 'New Brexit insurance clause' (*Airfinance Journal*, 19 June 2017).
12 International Air Transport Association, *The Impact of 'BREXIT' on UK Air Transport* (IATA, 2016) 3.

gising for the parties and catalyse them into being more conciliatory than in typical talks. This applies mainly to the UK, which has more to lose if the deal fails, at least as regards aviation.

Probably the quickest (and a readily available) solution for a future relationship between the EU and the UK would be through the EEA framework.[13] Once outside the EU, the UK could re-join EFTA,[14] which it left in 1972 upon joining the EEC (now EU). As an EFTA member state, it would be able to join the EEA agreement.[15] The UK's participation in the EEA would allow the application of EU law including the aviation *acquis* (with some modifications) to be extended to the UK. It would resolve most of the aforementioned problems in UK-EU27 relations in areas which are now governed by EU primary and derived law,[16] including UK participation in EASA, though without voting rights.[17] However, even participation in EFTA/ the EEA would not fix the problems in UK-third party aviation relations currently governed by EU-based agreements.[18]

Nonetheless, the UK's current political position in Brexit negotiations is at odds with its participation in the EEA. The UK government claims it will endeavour to ensure free trade with European markets, although will not seek to adopt a model already enjoyed by other countries. It also claims that it intends to restore the UK's full legislative powers and end jurisdiction of the CJEU, since it prefers traditional international arbitration instruments.[19]

13 For the role of the EEA in aviation and the impact of Brexit on this framework, see Chapter 1.4.1 of this book.
14 This accession would be subject to the EFTA Council decision. See Article 56 of the Convention establishing the European Free Trade Association, done at Stockholm on 4 January 1960, UNTS, Vol 370, No 5266, entered into force on 3 May 1960 (as amended in Vaduz on 21 June 2001).
15 This possibility is envisioned in Article 128 of the Agreement on the European Economic Area. However, such accession is subject to an agreement between EEA contracting parties and requires ratification or approval by these parties.
16 However, this would not happen automatically. EU law requires adaptation and incorporation into the EEA framework and implementation in EEA states. See A Scheving Thorsteinsson, 'Air Transport and the Agreement on the European Economic Area' (2015) 40(4–5) *Air & Space Law* 299, 305–309.
17 See Chapter 15 of this book.
18 EU external relations are generally not a part of the EEA agreement and EFTA/EEA member states participate only in selected EU-third party instruments. For a detailed discussion, see A Scheving Thorsteinsson, 'Air Transport and the Agreement on the European Economic Area' (2015) 40(4–5) *Air & Space Law* 299, 317–329.
19 Note that EU laws are incorporated into the EEA framework, whereas EFTA member states are subject to the surveillance of the EFTA Surveillance Authority and supervision of the EFTA court. For the UK Government position see HM Government, *The United Kingdom's exit from and new partnership with the European Union* (Cm 9417, 2017). Furthermore, the UK's position paper on trade policy is silent about EFTA membership, see Department for International Trade, *Preparing for our future UK trade policy* (Cm 9470, 2017).

Until the agreement for a future relationship between the EU and the UK is completed, nothing can be precluded; however, it seems more likely that the UK-EU27 relationship will be based on a separate comprehensive trade deal. For reasons mentioned previously, it is also questionable if the UK would accept an arrangement based on the EU-Swiss pattern.[20]

Notwithstanding the legal model of the agreement on a future relationship between the EU and the UK, the general scope of this arrangement may already be inferred from the EU and UK guidelines on Brexit. The European Council has envisioned this pact as a wide-ranging free trade agreement including trade in services and acknowledging the fact that the EU and the UK will no longer share a common regulatory, supervisory, enforcement and judiciary framework. The air transport services arrangement shall be aimed to ensure continued connectivity between the UK and the EU, which could be achieved, *inter alia*, through an air transport agreement, combined with aviation safety and security agreements. The agreement shall also ensure a level playing field in order to prevent possible UK legal dumping with respect to, *inter alia*, competition, state aid, tax and social, environmental and regulatory measures and practices.[21] The UK guidelines recognise that the agreement shall be designed for the benefit of the common systems and frameworks that currently enable free trade, and that it may take in elements of current single market arrangements in certain areas.[22] However, the EU has already warned that it will not allow for 'cherry picking' through the UK's participation in the EU single market based on a sector-by-sector approach.[23]

As regards the aviation sector, Part II of this book points to Brexit-relevant areas which will need to be considered in the UK-EU27 negotiations. Most of these issues are aviation-specific and shall be a part of Brexit aviation talks. However, some aviation-related issues are cross-sectoral and will not be directly discussed in aviation negotiations (e.g. fair competition, tariffs and trans-border employment). In this context, the existing legal framework in the form of the ECAA agreement offers a ready and comprehensive solution to address almost all aviation-specific issues in UK-EU relations,[24]

---

20 Switzerland has not entered the EEA agreement, but instead has concluded several sectoral agreements with the EU, including the air transport agreement. However, this agreement incorporates EU law and brings some matters under the CJEU's jurisdiction. See also Chapter 1.4.1 of this book.

21 European Council, 'European Council (Art. 50) (23 March 2018) – Guidelines' (EUCO XT 20001/18, 23 March 2018).

22 HM Government, *The United Kingdom's exit from and new partnership with the European Union* (Cm 9417, 2017) 35.

23 European Council, 'European Council (Art. 50) (23 March 2018) – Guidelines' (EUCO XT 20001/18, 23 March 2018) 3.

24 For the general scope and legal model of ECAA agreement, see Chapter 1.4.1 of this book.

including economic regulation, fair competition, safety and security, air navigation, the environment, social issues and consumer protection. To take advantage of this option, the UK would need to re-join the ECAA,[25] since the ECAA agreement will stop applying to the UK after Brexit.[26] Re-joining the ECAA would not only help to arrange the UK's aviation relations with the EU27, but also with eight other ECAA member states. It would also not preclude the UK's possible participation in the EEA. For these reasons, the UK government ought to consider the ECAA option and should not be discouraged by the fact that the ECAA framework incorporates EU aviation laws. Given the peculiarities of present aviation regulation, namely the EASA system and the SES programme, the incorporation mechanism suits the needs of the industry well and does not appear to cross any political red lines, especially seeing as the UK government did not preclude adoption of some elements of the current single market arrangements. What may cross a line though, is that the ECAA agreement leads to CJEU supervision.

From a political standpoint, the least controversial post-Brexit solution would be a bespoke aviation agreement between the UK and the EU27. It seems that the Euromed aviation agreements[27] have forged a pattern that could be useful for UK-EU27 relations, too. Accordingly, a bespoke agreement could take a threefold approach, where some issues are dealt with directly in the agreement, some are governed by the association agreement and some are regulated by reference to EU laws. Market access issues including traffic rights, ownership and control, investment and other airline rights could be governed by standard clauses typical of bilateral air services agreements, though preferably in a liberal manner to the extent possible. As regards cross-sector issues, in particular fair competition and state aid, the agreement could refer to the main agreement on a future relationship between the EU and the UK, which would certainly need to cover these issues. Regulatory cooperation in respect of aviation safety and security, air traffic management, environmental protection, air carrier liability, protection of personal data, CRS and social aspects could be subject to existing EU laws or, subject to approval by a joint committee, their replacements. This arrangement could also allow the UK to participate in EASA (although

---

25 This possibility is envisaged in Article 32 of the ECAA agreement. It is subject to the requirement that the acceding state has established or is establishing a framework of close economic cooperation with the EU. It seems that this requirement shall be satisfied by the agreement on a future relationship between the EU and the UK. However, re-joining the ECAA would be a time-consuming process including an amendment to the ECAA agreement that would need to be ratified or approved by the EU and 36 state parties. Note that it took over 11 years for the original ECAA agreement to enter into force.

26 See Chapter 1.4.1 of this book.

27 For these agreements, see Chapter 1.4.2 of this book.

without voting rights), in the SES initiative and in the SESAR programme. The surveillance of the agreement could be vested in the joint committee and, if consultations on this forum fail, a traditional dispute resolution mechanism could be launched.

The schedule just outlined is probably in line with the UK's expectations.[28] However, within this model, the EU27 may be reluctant to exchange some market access rights. Remarkably, the EU has exchanged rights such as cabotage and the Seventh Freedom, and has liberalised ownership and control and investment regimes, only within frameworks which ensure wide acceptance of EU laws and the jurisdiction of the CJEU, or of the laws and court of an equivalent body (e.g. EEA, ECAA). Hence, it is unlikely that the EU27 would now make an exception, especially for a country exiting the Union. Importantly, this is not only a matter of political principles. It must be acknowledged that there are considerable business forces within the EU27 that will push for a principled approach against the UK. Those EU27 airlines whose ownership structures will not be upset by Brexit and whose operations in the UK rely on the Third and Fourth Freedoms will insist on limiting market access only to these freedoms, and will welcome the reintroduction of the national ownership and control requirement on the UK's part. This stance has already been adopted by some EU27 legacy carriers[29] and even seems to have received a silent endorsement from their main counterpart in the UK.[30]

Political interests at the EU27 member state level may also interfere with Brexit negotiations. Importantly, the European Council Brexit guidelines clarify that, after the UK leaves the EU, no agreement between the EU

---

28 Should the incorporation of EU laws into the agreement be too far reaching, there is still an option for a traditional bilateral air services agreement between the UK and EU27, possibly modelled on the EU-US and EU-Canada agreements. However, this solution would not secure matters currently dealt with within the EASA system and SES framework, and thus would burden the UK with resolving these issues unilaterally.

29 Lufthansa, Air France-KLM, SAS, Croatia Airlines and TAP Portugal have called for regulatory convergence between the EU and the UK as a precondition for UK airlines' access to the internal aviation market. See Centre for Asia Pacific Aviation, 'The great Brexit aviation debate. A transition deal is needed to avoid disaster for UK airlines' (*CAPA*, 1 November 2017) <https://centreforaviation.com/analysis/reports/the-great-brexit-aviation-debate-a-transition-deal-is-needed-to-avoid-disaster-for-uk-airlines-380522> accessed 15 June 2018.

30 See also Chapter 3.1 of this book. This tactic is meant to hamper competition from LCC operators which are highly reliant on cabotage, the Seventh Freedom and the EU ownership and control principle. However, it seems short-sighted and, as mentioned, it may well turn into a lose-lose scenario. Ultimately, the available LCC short-haul capacity will not be easily erased from the market and eventually, with the LCCs still operating or not, it will be mainly relocated to the only available European Third and Fourth Freedom routes, leading to obvious price erosion in this market segment.

and the UK may apply to the territory of Gibraltar without an agreement between Spain and the UK.[31] On the one hand, being the primary destination for British tourists and being home to the IAG holding, Spain would be interested in a liberal UK-EU27 aviation arrangement. On the other hand, Spanish diplomats have already warned that Madrid will not accept any post-Brexit deal that would imply recognition of the legal right of the UK to the territory on which Gibraltar's international airport is situated.[32] The previously mentioned industry and political positions indicate that both UK and EU negotiators should be double alert and should draft the future agreement having in mind the long-term benefits for the whole sector and the general public, not the temporary interests of certain airlines or political forces that will surely be vocal.

However, it must be made clear that even if the negotiators reach consensus over a far-reaching, liberal arrangement, the agreement on a future relationship between the EU and the UK will not solve all post-Brexit regulatory problems discussed earlier in this book. The UK-EU27 agreement will only work for aviation relations between the UK and EU27 member states and would only give UK airlines traffic rights in these relations. Within the EFTA/EEA or ECAA frameworks, the UK could also guarantee some additional European traffic rights, although not all of the rights currently supported by EU air carrier status.[33] A similar problem will concern airline ownership and control criteria in post-Brexit agreements. Finally, the UK-EU27 deal will not encompass EU-third party relations governed by EU comprehensive and horizontal agreements.[34] This is because there is

31 Paragraph 24 of European Council, 'Guidelines following the United Kingdom's Notification under Article 50 TEU' (EUCO XT 20004/17, 29 April 2017).

32 See P McClean and A Barker, 'Gibraltar: Dispute over rock puts negotiators in a hard place' *Financial Times* (London, 13 February 2017) 5. An earlier version appeared online, but is subscription only: P McClean and T Buck, 'Gibraltar poses threat to post-Brexit aviation access' *Financial Times* (London, 12 February 2017) <www.ft.com/content/a62b292a-ef99-11e6-930f-061b01e23655> accessed 15 June 2018. Some commentators suggest that this issue should be treated seriously, since Spain already has a tradition of holding up EU aviation initiatives due to the Gibraltar problem and may be willing to invoke this issue in Brexit negotiations for political reasons. See B Humphreys, 'Brexit and Aviation: All Clear Now?' (2016) XV(3) *Aviation & Space Journal* 30, 35.

33 This is because the EU aviation *acquis*, the EAA agreement, the Swiss-EU agreement and the ECAA agreement are relatively independent regimes that are collectively more beneficial for EU airlines in terms of traffic rights. See J Walulik, *Progressive Commercialization of Airline Governance Culture* (Abingdon, New York: Routledge 2017) 221–222. As regards EFTA-EEA member states, note that the EFTA convention, the Swiss-EU agreement and the EEA agreement are also autonomous in terms of traffic rights, see A Scheving Thorsteinsson, 'Air Transport and the Agreement on the European Economic Area' (2015) 40(4–5) *Air & Space Law* 299, 314–315.

34 The UK will need to arrange for these aviation relations itself; see Chapter 19 of this book.

no single multilateral instrument to harmonise airline nationality and traffic rights between the EU and its partners and between those partners themselves within a single aviation market.

If the EU gets no mandate to negotiate a post-Brexit UK-EU27 arrangement or such arrangement fails, the relations between the UK and EU27 member states will be regulated by revived bilateral agreements. However, as argued, these agreements will not automatically regain their previous wording after Brexit and may be unsuitable to uphold current traffic levels.[35] In such case, the UK may wish to negotiate new bilateral agreements or renegotiate existing bilateral agreements with EU27 member states. However, this possibility will be limited by EU competences. First, intra-community services performed by British carriers (Fifth and Seventh and cabotage services) will need to be fully subject to EU laws and, as to these services, bilateral agreements cannot include provisions conflicting with these laws. Second, provisions of bilateral agreements cannot depart from those EU rules which are directly applicable to foreign air carriers (e.g. CRS, slot allocation).[36] Finally, bilateral negotiations between the UK and EU27 member states will be subject to limitations arising from regulation 847/2008.[37]

---

35 See Chapters 1.4 and 3 of this book.
36 These kind of limitations have been confirmed in the CJEU's 'open skies' judgements, see Judgments of the Court of 5 November 2002 – Cases: C-466/98 *Commission v UK* [2002] ECR I-9427; C-467/98 *Commission v Denmark* [2002] ECR I-9519; C-468/98 *Commission v Sweden* [2002] ECR I-9575; C-469/98 *Commission v Finland* [2002] ECR I-9627; C-471/98 *Commission v Belgium* [2002] ECR I-9681; C-472/98 *Commission v Luxembourg* [2002] ECR I-9741; C-475/98 *Commission v Austria* [2002] ECR I-9797; C-476/98 *Commission v Germany* [2002] ECR I-9855. However, any agreements between the UK and EU27 member states would require a case-by-case analysis. See also L Vrbaski, 'Flying into the Unknown: The UK's Air Transport Relations with the European Union and Third Countries Following "Brexit"' (2016) 41(6) *Air & Space Law* 421, 437–439.
37 See Chapter 1.4 of this book.

18 UK domestic forum

Brexit will engage the UK legislature on several occasions. First, both the withdrawal agreement and the agreement on a future relationship between the EU and the UK, mentioned in the previous chapter, will need to be approved by the UK Parliament. Second, although Brexit itself is a matter of EU law and is ruled by the procedure established in Article 50 TEU, it also involves repeal of the ECA that will become redundant when the UK ceases to be a party to the Treaties. For this purpose, the European Union (Withdrawal) Act 2018 was passed on 26 June 2018.[1] However, the mere repeal of the ECA would leave significant gaps in the UK legal system. Not least, it would make void any UK secondary legislation made under section 2(2) ECA in order to implement EU laws. It would also end the supremacy of EU law and the interpretation of law based on CJEU rulings in the UK. Therefore, the European Union (Withdrawal) Act 2018 offers further provisions to try to address these additional problems.

First, it preserves domestic secondary legislation enacted in order to implement EU laws. Second, it incorporates into UK domestic law all directly applicable EU legislation (in particular, regulations and decisions), along with the adaptations of EU law to the EEA regime. The act also anticipates that any rights, powers, liabilities, obligations, restrictions, remedies and procedures arising from EU law (other than those preserved or incorporated as previously stated) which are directly recognised and available in domestic law by virtue of section 2(1) ECA continue to be recognised and available in domestic law on and after Exit Day.

---

1 European Union (Withdrawal) Act 2018, 2018 ch 16. Note, however, that key provisions of this act, that are discussed in this book, come into force on such day as a Minister of the Crown may by regulations appoint; and different days may be appointed for different purposes (Section 25(4) of the act). Subject to the European Union (Withdrawal) Act 2018 (Commencement and Transitional Provisions) Regulations 2018, SI 2018/808 (ch 63), some selected provisions of the European Union (Withdrawal) Act 2018 have already entered into force on 4 July 2018, whereas other selected provisions will enter into force on Exit Day.

The intention is that the principle of the supremacy of EU law will continue to apply, however, only to enactments or rules of law passed or made before Exit Day and to their modifications, provided that application of the principle is consistent with the intention of the modification. As regards interpretation of law, the act envisages especially that retained EU case law and any retained general principles of EU law shall apply to the retained EU law. UK courts or tribunals shall not be bound by post-Brexit EU jurisprudence, although they may have regard to it if they consider it appropriate to do so. The Supreme Court and, in some instances, the High Court of Justiciary may depart from any retained EU case law, provided that they apply the same tests as they would apply in deciding whether to depart from their own case law.

All of this notwithstanding, a large part of the retained EU law, if unchanged, will not achieve the desired legal effect. In particular, the retained EU law may not operate effectively because the UK will simply not be an EU member state or because it requires the involvement of an EU institution or reciprocal arrangements that will not be guaranteed post-Brexit. Moreover, it may include references which are no longer appropriate or provisions which have no practical application or are otherwise redundant. For these types of occasions, the European Union (Withdrawal) Act 2018 empowers a Minister of the Crown to make secondary legislation (regulations) to eliminate deficiencies and ensure the proper functioning of UK laws as well as to ensure post-Brexit compliance with international obligations and the proper implementation of the withdrawal agreement. The Minister is to be so empowered until the expiry of a two-year term beginning with Exit Day. Any changes to the retained legislation which exceed this described delegation of powers[2] or which are to be enacted after this delegation expires will require an Act of Parliament. Primary legislation will also be the right way to change any acts of Parliament which implement EU law,[3] as well as secondary legislation made under such acts.

There have been some controversies concerning devolved legislatures, powers delegated to the government, and Parliamentary scrutiny of subordinate legislation. A detailed discussion of these cross-sector issues would exceed the scope of this book. However, it is worth noting here that the act should correspond with the negotiated withdrawal agreement. In this context, there is a lack of clarity around the relation between the method employed in the act to incorporate EU law into the British legal system and

---

2 For instance, changes constituting implementation of the agreement on a future relationship between the EU and the UK.

3 However, Schedule 8 Part 2 to the Act already proposes changes to some selected parts of UK primary legislation.

the UK's obligations arising from the Draft Withdrawal Agreement concerning the application of EU law in the transition period. The current act also does not explain how any changes to EU law which enter into force in the transition period are to be applied in the UK.[4] These issues will have to be solved by British lawmakers.

Unfortunately, even if properly managed, the incorporation of EU law into the UK legal regime will not resolve all problems concerning aviation. This process will fill the legal gaps and will sustain legal foundations necessary for the functioning of UK civil aviation in respect of activities which are now governed by EU law (e.g. air product certification, air carrier services, air navigation services). The transitional and grandfather provisions will also help to protect in the UK some rights and obligations acquired under the current EU aviation regime, and facilitate ongoing court and administrative proceedings.[5] However, the unilaterally applied EU aviation law will not be able to fully shield rights and obligations in any relations which involve EU27 member states (e.g. traffic rights, recognition of licences and certificates, SES etc.). These issues could only be addressed in a future UK-EU27 aviation deal. The mere incorporation of EU law in the UK will also not automatically solve the practical issues concerning the takeover of executive powers by the UK.[6] British legislation will obviously also be unable to solve problems in aviation relations with third parties.

What is more, as one commentator put it, to incorporate EU law in domestic legislation leads to the question: what does the UK gain by Brexit?[7] As regards civil aviation, it will be extremely hard, if possible at all, for the UK to cherry-pick those parts of the aviation *acquis* which it wishes to retain. First, in many cases, such a policy would exceed the government's delegated powers to eliminate deficiencies in retained EU law and, thus, would involve acts of Parliament which would make it very time consuming. Second, the nature of the aviation business means that it cannot be

---

4 Note that the preliminarily accepted Article 122(3) of the Draft Withdrawal Agreement provides that during the transition period, the applicable EU law shall produce in respect of and in the UK the same legal effects as those which it produces within the EU and its member states, and shall be interpreted and applied in accordance with the same methods and general principles as those applicable within the EU.

5 However, according to Schedule 8 Part 3 of the European Union (Withdrawal) Act 2018, these provisions are subject i.a. to the provisions on the retention of existing EU law (Sections 2–6 of the act), including possible post-Brexit adaptations of this law.

6 See Chapter 15 of this book.

7 R Williams, 'Brexit and international trade: the way forward – or is it back?' (Brexit: The Legal & Operational Implications, Royal Aeronautical Society Seminar, London, 26 January 2017).

fully organised within a single jurisdiction.[8] Consequently, the UK will still have to rely on arrangements with the EU27 and/or its member states in many respects. Finally, with or without a UK-EU27 aviation deal, the UK will likely have no choice but to replicate some EU legislation for practical reasons, although it will have no influence on the shape of this legislation.[9] Even so, over time, changes to the retained EU legislation in the UK and the amendments to EU law at the EU27 level will inevitably lead to discrepancies between both regimes.

8 If there are some issues usually regulated in air services agreements that the UK could regulate unilaterally, these would only be concessions to EU27 member states; e.g. the UK could grant EU27 carriers the privilege to operate cabotage services within the UK. It could also grandfather or even sustain the EU air carrier membership and control regime in the UK.
9 Due to the advanced integration of the European aerospace industry, for instance, it is questionable if UK laws could depart significantly from the EU aviation safety framework.

19 UK-third party forum

Part I of this book indicates that Brexit will have impact on several types of legal acts including international agreements. Many of these agreements concern the UK's relations with parties other than EU member states. In such case, neither a UK-EU27 arrangement nor UK unilateral actions will be sufficient, and post-Brexit solutions will need to involve negotiations with third parties. As discussed earlier, the impact of Brexit on UK-third party relations will depend on the nature and wording of current international agreements entered into by the EU and its member states or by the EU itself.

Current comprehensive international arrangements for air services between the EU and third parties, including the EEA agreement, the EU-Swiss aviation agreement, the ECAA agreement, CAA agreements, Euromed aviation agreements and vertical air transport agreements, will cease to apply to the UK after Brexit. This will bring about mixed results. On the one hand, in some relations old UK-third party bilateral air services agreements will be revived in whole. On the other hand, some UK bilateral agreements have been modified or superseded by the EU-third party regimes and will not regain their original wording.[1] Finally, in some cases, absent an EU-third party agreement, there will be no air services arrangement between the UK and the third party concerned. However, even if fully revived, the old British bilateral agreements will often be ill-suited to today's aviation market.[2] Therefore, in many cases, the UK will need to negotiate new air services agreements or renegotiate its existing agreements with the current EU aviation partners.

It must be recognised that the scope of air services agreements to be renegotiated by the UK depends on the model of future UK-EU27 relations.

---

1 See Chapter 1.5 of this book.
2 The most apparent contradiction is probably between the restrictive Bermuda II agreement to be revived and the huge UK-US air traffic.

Should this arrangement be based on the UK's participation in the EEA and/or ECAA, the task for the UK would be simpler. Such an option would secure not only most of the UK's European third-party aviation relations, but could also enable its continued access to the EU-US air transport agreement.[3] However, just as in the case of UK-EU27 relations, none of the possible configurations for the UK's third-party aviation relations post-Brexit will be able to secure all traffic rights which British air carriers now enjoy as EU airlines. Revived or new bilateral agreements will usually support Third–Fourth and sometimes Fifth Freedom traffic, whereas participation in the EEA and/or ECAA could add some extra Seventh Freedom and cabotage rights. Once again, the LCCs will be vitally interested in liberal UK-third party regimes, while airlines concentrated on hub-and-spoke networks may be satisfied with traditional bilateral frameworks.

Another sphere in third-party relations that will be problematic for the UK after Brexit is the UK's bilateral air services agreements which embrace EU ownership and control clauses added either by means of EU horizontal agreements or on the UK's initiative. As mentioned, Brexit will render them highly asymmetric to the detriment of the UK. Unfortunately, the construction of the EU ownership and control clauses is such that even the UK's participation in the EEA would not solve the discussed problem.[4] Consequently, Britain will be forced to renegotiate all such bilateral agreements after Brexit.[5]

An additional group of Brexit-affected international instruments consists in agreements concerning aviation safety and security.[6] These agreements, which have been concluded by the EU within its competences, will not apply to the UK after Brexit. The UK will need to consider signing new agreements or updating its existing agreements with third parties in this respect. Some multilateral mixed agreements – such as the CTC with its aircraft protocol, and GATS – will still apply to Britain, but may require additional declarations or commitments on the part of the UK after Brexit.

---

3 The EU-US open skies agreement was expanded to non-EU EEA member states Iceland and Norway in 2011. If it were an EEA member state, the UK could take the same course and re-enter the EU-US agreement.
4 The clauses included in EU horizontal agreements and the EU standard clauses for inclusion in bilateral air service agreements specify that majority ownership and effective control of designated air carriers shall be vested in EU member states and/or EFTA states (Iceland, Liechtenstein, Norway and Switzerland) and/or nationals of such states. However, the designation itself is conditional upon establishment in the territory of the designating EU member state under the TFEU and the effective regulatory control of the airline being exerted by an EU member state.
5 See Chapter 1.5 of this book.
6 See Chapter 1.4.4 of this book.

There are also mixed free trade agreements covering some aviation issues that will cease to apply to the UK post-Brexit. The UK will need to negotiate new instruments for their replacement.[7]

The UK government has argued that Brexit will unlock the potential in UK-third party relations[8] including aviation relations.[9] It is perhaps true, though, for several practical reasons that it will be extremely hard – if it is possible at all – for the UK to develop this potential. First, although Britain is the largest aviation market in Europe, it will not have the same bargaining power in international relations as the 500-million population bloc comprised of 28 nations.[10] Second, negotiation timing will be unfortunate for the UK. A huge part of the UK's bilateral aviation relations will be disturbed by Brexit, and there will be no multilateral option at the ICAO or WTO level to lean on after quitting the EU. Consequently, Britain will have to simultaneously negotiate and complete aviation deals with a vast number of states. Where it fails to do so before Exit Day, in many instances the parties would have to rely on comity and reciprocity until an arrangement is reached. Though comity and reciprocity is nothing exceptional in aviation relations, it would be highly uncomfortable to have a large part of international traffic based on such unstable principles. It is also unlikely that third parties will not try to take advantage of the coercive circumstances surrounding Britain in the aforementioned negotiations.[11] Furthermore, to advance its aviation market by means of developing third-party relations, the UK would urgently need to improve the capacity of its hubs which serve long-haul traffic, especially Heathrow.[12] Finally, the UK's third-party relations may also be limited by its future arrangements with the EU27.

7 See Chapters 1.6–1.7 of this book.
8 See Department for International Trade, *Preparing for our future UK trade policy* (White paper, Cm 9470, 2017).
9 Chris Grayling claimed that leaving the EU gives the UK more freedom to make its own aviation agreements with other countries beyond Europe, for instance, whereas Lord Callanan emphasized the role of air traffic with China and India and of establishing links with growing economies outside the EU. See: HC Deb 23 November 2016, vol 617, col 952; 'Transport minister insists UK will get "open air" deal with EU' (*TravelMole*, 29 June 2017) <www.travelmole.com/news_feature.php?news_id=2027743> accessed 15 June 2018.
10 International Air Transport Association, *The Impact of 'BREXIT' on UK Air Transport* (IATA 2016) 4.
11 There have already been reports of a tough US stance in ongoing aviation negotiations with the UK, see: K Manson, A Barker and T Powley, 'US offers UK inferior open skies deal after Brexit' *Financial Times* (London, 5 March 2018) <www.ft.com/content/9461157c-1f97-11e8-9efc-0cd3483b8b80> accessed 15 June 2018 (online only, subscription required); T. McEnaney, 'Blue sky between airlines on Brexit' *The Times* (London, 14 March 2018) 33.
12 To enable further development at Heathrow a government statement (*Airports National Policy Statement: new runway capacity and infrastructure at airports in the South East of England*, Department of Transport, June 2018) has been presented to the Parliament.

In this context, it is worth mentioning that according to the preliminarily agreed provisions of the Draft Withdrawal Agreement, within the transition period the UK would be bound by the obligations stemming from the international agreements concluded by the EU, or by member states acting on its behalf, or by the EU and its member states acting jointly.[13] A footnote to this passage explains that the EU will notify the other parties to these agreements that during the transition period, the UK is to be treated as a member state for the purposes of these agreements. Whereas the UK's commitment to be bound by EU-third party agreements seems clear, neither this commitment nor the EU's notification addressed to third states is sufficient to ensure that those states will continue to apply their agreements with the EU to the UK during the transition period. Once more, it seems this practice will be subject to comity and reciprocity.[14] This position will be insecure for the UK, especially if it waives the right to implement its own agreements with third parties before the end of the transition period.[15]

It has been approved, and was designated as a national policy by the Secretary of State for Transport on 26 June 2018. However, the construction of the third runway at Heathrow will involve environmental issues, and is controversial in this respect. For the debate on the third Heathrow runway, see: L Butcher and others, 'Heathrow expansion' (Briefing Paper No CBP1136, House of Commons Library 2018).

13 See Article 124(1) of Draft Withdrawal Agreement of 19 March 2018, TF50 (2018) 35.

14 It seems that this is what UK Government hopes for, see *Technical note: International agreements during the implementation period* (HM Government, 8 February 2018).

15 According to preliminarily agreed Article 124(4) of Draft Withdrawal Agreement of 19 March 2018, TF50 (2018) 35 the UK may negotiate, sign and ratify international agreements entered into in its own capacity in the areas of exclusive competence of the EU, provided those agreements do not enter into force or apply during the transition period, unless so authorised by the EU.

Conclusions

Many commentators compare Brexit to accession negotiations in reverse. Whereas this notion may be true in reference to the departure from Treaty freedoms and the single market, it does not really illustrate the complexity of post-Brexit air law issues. The high scope of EU-level legal harmonisation and technical cooperation in aviation and the very wide reliance on EU-third party instruments in this sector make one think of Brexit in aviation rather like reinventing large parts of air law: drafting a new regime for economic regulation of air services; re-establishing legal, administrative and technical frameworks for aviation safety and air navigation services; and renegotiating a large part of the UK's bilateral aviation agreements with third parties, to mention just three.

Given the scale of the Brexit complications in aviation, it would probably be valid to consider if this process may be reversed. Article 50 TEU is silent on this matter. However, according to Article 68 VCLT, a notification of withdrawing from a treaty may be revoked at any time before it takes effect, and there seems to be nothing in the TEU which would limit this right.[1] This implies that from the treaty perspective, the UK is free to revoke its notification of withdrawal from the EU before Exit Day as defined in Article 50(3) TEU.[2] It seems that a possible notification of revocation could take the same form as the withdrawal notice and could also be transmitted to the European Council. The consent of the EU or its member states to such a declaration would not be required, at least until the Withdrawal Agreement is concluded. It is debatable if under the UK's constitutional arrangements

---

1 Not least Article 50(5) TEU, which speaks of rejoining the EU. This provision is addressed to a state which already has withdrawn from the EU.
2 The purpose of Article 68 VCLT suggests that the 'effect' referred to in this provision shall be understood as the ordinary effect of the notification of withdrawal (i.e. that the treaty ceases to apply to the party concerned) not as any effect related to such notification (e.g. commencement of withdrawal negotiations).

the revocation of withdrawal would require authorisation by a prior Act of Parliament as the notification of withdrawal did.[3] Certainly, on and after Exit Day, no revocation would be possible. At this stage, the UK could still re-join the EU, although it is unlikely that it could secure opt-outs comparable to the current ones.

Notwithstanding legal matters, Brexit reversal seems unlikely from a political standpoint, at least without a change of government or a second referendum in the UK. What is more, managing Brexit is not only about aviation and its unique legal challenges. However, even in this sector, there is no consensus as to coping with these challenges. As mentioned, there are interest groups in aviation which believe that their business is largely Brexit-immune and which would welcome post-Brexit legal restrictions on their competitors' activities. There are also some purely political convictions in the UK and on the continent which seem to preclude a far-reaching post-Brexit aviation deal. On the one hand, there is the British objection to any kind of scrutiny by the CJEU, even in technical matters such as aviation safety. On the other hand, there is the equally destructive 'punishment doctrine' in the EU which holds that Brexit should lead to a limitation of the UK's rights, at least in terms of access to European markets.

The Brexit negotiators face a very hard task of setting aside economic particularisms and overcoming political obstacles. Thirty years of European aviation liberalisation is at stake. The emergence of the EU single air market would not have been possible without the British experience and initiative, and its later development without the UK's expertise in aviation safety and air navigation.[4] The current state of this market also depends on the huge British market attracting numerous carriers, including Europe's price leaders. Continuation of this success story will not be possible without an open UK-EU27 aviation deal. Both the EU's external aviation policy and the UK's post-Brexit trade strategy are based on liberal foundations. Therefore,

---

3 In the case of the withdrawal, the requirement for such authorisation was supported mainly by the fact that this process involves a change of domestic law; see the Supreme Court's judgment of 24 January 2017: *R (Miller) v Secretary of State for Exiting the European Union* [2017] UKSC 5. In this context, revocation of the notification of a withdrawal which has not yet taken effect will not bring about any change in UK domestic laws. Note also that the European Union (Notification of Withdrawal) Act 2017, 2017 ch 9, allows the Prime Minister to notify the UK's intention to withdraw from the EU but does not oblige her to do so. That notwithstanding, in the case of a Brexit reversal, an Act of Parliament would be required to repeal the European Union (Withdrawal) Act 2018.

4 It was the UK which pioneered and promoted air transport liberalisation and privatisation in Europe, see: SJ Fox, 'Brexit: A Bolt from the Blue! – Red Sky in the Morning?' (2016) 16 *Issues in Aviation Law and Policy* 83, 97; B Humphreys, 'Brexit and Aviation: All Clear Now?' (2016) XV(3) *Aviation & Space Journal* 30, 33–34.

there is no reason why a future arrangement between these two powers should bring about market restrictions.

One thing seems certain. The single air market is a common achievement of European nations and a common asset of the whole European economy and of hundreds of millions of consumers. In the long run, a failure to deliver a true open skies environment between the UK and the EU27 post-Brexit will be a victory not for one or another part of the European aviation industry, but only for those few who seek to capitalise on the destabilisation that Brexit has brought on both sides of the English Channel.

Bibliography

ADS, 2017 'Industry Facts & Figures. A Guide to the UK's Aerospace, Defence, Security & Space Sectors' (ADS Group Limited 2017)

Airport Operators Association, 'New Aviation Agreements to Underpin a Truly Global Britain' (*AOA*, 17 January 2017) <www.aoa.org.uk/new-aviation-agreements-to-underpin-a-truly-global-britain/> accessed 7 August 2018

Airport Operators Association, 'Building a Strong Aviation Partnership with the EU' (*AOA*, 29 March 2017) <www.aoa.org.uk/building-a-strong-aviation-partnership-with-the-eu/> accessed 7 August 2018

Airports Council International Europe, 'Brexit & Aviation. Market Interdependence and Economic Value' (ACI Europe 2017)

Airports Council International 'Europe, The Ownership of Europe's Airports 2016' (ACI Europe 2017)

Bartels L, 'The UK's status in the WTO after Brexit' (article, 23 September 2016) <www.peacepalacelibrary.nl/ebooks/files/407396411.pdf> accessed 15 June 2018

Biondi A, 'The First on the Flight Home: The Sad Story of State Aid Control in the Brexit Age' (2016) 27 *King's Law Journal* 442

Business, Energy and Industrial Strategy Committee, 'The impact of Brexit on the aerospace sector' (HC 2017–19, 380)

Butcher L and others, 'Heathrow expansion' (House of Commons Library Briefing Paper, No CBP1136, 2018)

Callan B, 'Defense High and Low Roads After Brexit' (2016) 178(14) *Aviation Week & Space Technology*

Center for Asia Pacific Aviation, 'Brexit and aviation Part 1: Open Pandora's box and anything can happen. But status quo is likely' (*CAPA*, 27 June 2016) <https://centreforaviation.com/insights/analysis/brexit-and-aviation-part-1-open-pandoras-box-and-anything-can-happen-but-status-quo-is-likely-288477> accessed 7 August 2018

Center for Asia Pacific Aviation, 'Brexit and aviation Part 3: Importance of Asian models and liberalisation moves will be accelerated' (*CAPA*, 28 June 2016) <https://centreforaviation.com/insights/analysis/brexit-and-aviation-part-3-importance-of-asian-models-and-liberalisation-moves-will-be-accelerated-288736> accessed 7 August 2018

Center for Asia Pacific Aviation, 'Airport investment: The top 10 investors from CAPA's Global Airport Investors Database' (*CAPA*, 9 August 2017) <https://centreforaviation.com/insights/analysis/airport-investment-the-top-10-investors-from-capas-global-airport-investors-database-360459> accessed 7 August 2018

Center for Asia Pacific Aviation, 'The great Brexit aviation debate. A transition deal is needed to avoid disaster for UK airlines' (*CAPA*, 1 November 2017) <https://centreforaviation.com/insights/analysis/the-great-brexit-aviation-debate-a-transition-deal-is-needed-to-avoid-disaster-for-uk-airlines-380522> accessed 7 August 2018

Cronrath E-M and others, 'Brexit – Auswirkungen auf den deutschen und europäischen Luftverkehr' (2016) 96(9) *Wirtschaftsdienst* 675

Delimatsis P, The Evolution of the EU External Trade Policy in Services – CETA, TTIP, and TiSA after Brexit (2017) 20 *Journal of International Economic Law* 583

Doganis R, 'UK departure opens Pandora's box' (2017) 33(5) *Airline Business*

Fox SJ, 'Brexit: A Bolt from the Blue! – Red Sky in the Morning?' (2016) 16 *Issues in Aviation Law and Policy* 83

Goodwin A, 'Brexit – Customs borders will impose costs and delays' (2017) 41(2) *Economic Outlook* 11

Gray K, 'CTC in Europe assessment of ratifications to date and implications of Brexit on the ratification by the UK' (2016) 5(1) *Cape Town Convention Journal* 1

Hadjyianni I, 'The UK and the World: Environmental Law' in PJ Birkinshaw and A Biondi (eds), *Britain Alone! The Implications and Consequences of the United Kingdom Exit from the EU* (Wolters Kluwer 2016)

Haines A, 'The future of open skies post-Brexit' (GAD speech, Civil Aviation Authority, 1 December 2016)

Harper L, 'What is at stake for easyJet and Ryanair from Brexit' (*Flight Global*, 11 May 2017) <www.flightglobal.com/news/articles/analysis-what-is-at-stake-for-easyjet-and-ryanair-f-436638/> accessed 7 August 2018

Haylen A and Butcher L, *Airport slots* (House of Commons Library Briefing Paper, No CBP 488, 2017)

Hillion C, 'Brexit means Br(EEA)xit: The UK withdrawal from the EU and its implications for the EEA' (2018) 55(1) *Common Market Law Review* 135

Hofmann K, 'BMI Regional considers possible Brexit strategies' (*ATW Plus*, 28 March 2017) <http://atwonline.com/airlines/bmi-regional-considers-possible-brexit-strategies> accessed 7 August 2018

Humphreys B, 'Brexit and Aviation: All Clear Now?' (2016) XV(3) *The Aviation & Space Journal* 30

International Air Transport Association, *The Impact of 'BREXIT' on UK Air Transport* (IATA 2016)

International Air Transport Association, *Worldwide Slot Guidelines* (8th edn, IATA 2017)

Kierzenkowski R and others, 'The Economic Consequences of Brexit. A taxing Decision' (OECD Economic Policy Paper No 16, 2016)

Manson K, Barker A and Powley T, 'US offers UK inferior open skies deal after Brexit' *Financial Times* (London, 5 March 2018) <www.ft.com/content/9461157c-1f97-11e8-9efc-0cd3483b8b80> accessed 7 August 2018 (online only, subscription required)

McClean P and Barker A, 'UK airlines brought down to earth by Brexit' *Financial Times* (London, 13 February 2017) 5

McClean P and Barker A, 'Gibraltar: Dispute over rock puts negotiators in a hard place' *Financial Times* (London, 13 February 2017) 5

McEnaney T, 'Blue sky between airlines on Brexit' *The Times* (London, 14 March 2018) 33

Mueller L, 'New Brexit insurance clause' *Airfinance Journal*, 19 June 2017

Osborne T, 'Brexit Damage Control Plans for UK Aerospace and Defense' (*Aviation Week*, 1 July 2016) <http://aviationweek.com/defense/brexit-damage-control-plans-uk-aerospace-and-defense> accessed 7 August 2018 (online only, subscription required)

Osborne T, 'Brexit Dilemmas' (2016) 178(14) *Aviation Week & Space Technology* 42

Perry D, 'Dassault plays down Brexit fears over Anglo-French UCAV project' (*Flightglobal.com*, 10 March 2017) <www.flightglobal.com/news/articles/dassault-plays-down-brexit-fears-over-anglo-french-u-435036/> accessed 7 August 2018

Robinson T, 'Tailwind or turbulence? Brexit and UK aerospace' (Report from Royal Aeronautical Society Conference, London, 6 December 2016) <www.aerosociety.com/news/tailwind-or-turbulence-brexit-and-uk-aerospace/> accessed 7 August 2018

Scheving Thorsteinsson A, 'Air Transport and the Agreement on the European Economic Area' (2015) 40(4–5) *Air & Space Law* 299

Scotford E and Bowman M, 'Brexit and Environmental Law: Challenges and Opportunities' (2016) 27(3) *King's Law Journal* 416

Steinberger E, 'The WTO Treaty as a Mixed Agreement: Problems with the EC's and the EC Member States' Membership of the WTO' (2006) 14 *European Journal of International Law* 837

Thisdell D, 'Brexit casts shadow over UK aerospace' (*FlightGlobal*, 15 June 2017) <www.flightglobal.com/news/articles/analysis-brexit-casts-shadow-over-uk-aerospace-437582/> accessed 13 June 2018

'Transport minister insists UK will get "open air" deal with EU' (*TravelMole*, 29 June 2017) <www.travelmole.com/news_feature.php?news_id=2027743> accessed 7 August 2018

Vrbaski L, 'Flying into the Unknown: The UK's Air Transport Relations with the European Union and Third Countries Following "Brexit"' (2016) 41(6) *Air & Space Law* 421

Walulik J, *Progressive Commercialization of Airline Governance Culture* (Abingdon, New York: Routledge 2017)

Williams R, 'Brexit and international trade: the way forward – or is it back?' (Brexit: The Legal & Operational Implications, Royal Aeronautical Society Seminar, London, 26 January 2017)

Wiltshire J, 'An Economic View on Political Developments: Implications for Aviation' (Brexit: The Legal & Operational Implications, Royal Aeronautical Society Seminar, London, 26 January 2017)

Official documents

Commission, 'The EU's External Aviation Policy – Addressing Future Challenges' (Communication) COM/2012/0556 final

Commission and others, 'An Aviation Strategy for Europe' (Communication) COM/2015/0598 final

Council of the EU, Directives for the negotiation of an agreement with the United Kingdom of Great Britain and Northern Ireland setting out the arrangements for its withdrawal from the European Union, Brussels, 22.05.2017, XT 21016/17, ADD 1 REV 2

Council of the EU, Supplementary directives for the negotiation of an agreement with the United Kingdom of Great Britain and Northern Ireland setting out the arrangements for its withdrawal from the European Union, Brussels, 29.01.2018, XT 21004/18, ADD 1 REV 2

Draft Withdrawal Agreement of 19 March 2018, TF50 (2018) 35

Department for International Trade, *Preparing for our future UK trade policy* (Cm 9470, 2017)

Department for Transport, *Airports National Policy Statement: new runway capacity and infrastructure at airports in the South East of England* (HM Government 2018)

European Council, *Guidelines following the United Kingdom's notification under Article 50 TEU*, Brussels, 29.04.2017 (EUCO XT 20004/17), 15.12.2017 (EUCO XT 20011/17), 23.03.2018 (EUCO XT 20001/18)

HM Government, *The United Kingdom's exit from and new partnership with the European Union* (White Paper, Cm 9417, 2017)

HM Government, *Technical note: International agreements during the implementation period* (HM Government 2018)

'Joint statement from the negotiators of the European Union and the United Kingdom Government on progress of negotiations under Article 50 TEU on the United Kingdom's orderly withdrawal from the European Union', 19 June 2018, TF50 (2018) 52

Manual on the Regulation of International Air Transport, ICAO Doc 9626

Transport Committee, Oral evidence: Aviation and Brexit (HC 2017–2019, 531)

Court judgments

CJEU

Judgment of the Court of 30 April 1986 – Cases C-209–213/84 Ministère Public v Lucas Asjes and Others [1986] ECR 1425

Opinion No 1/94 of the Court of 15 November 1994, Competence of the Community to conclude international agreements concerning services and the protection of intellectual property – Article 228 (6) of the EC Treaty [1994] ECR I-5267

Judgments of the Court of 5 November 2002 – Cases: C-466/98, [2002] ECR I-09427; C-467/98 [2002] ECR I-09519; C-468/98, [2002] ECR I-09575; C-469/98, [2002] ECR I-09627; C-471/98, [2002] ECR I-09681; C-472/98, [2002] ECR I-09741; C-475/98, [2002] ECR I-09797; C-476/98, [2002] ECR I-09855 ('Open Skies')

UK

R (Miller) v Secretary of State for Exiting the European Union [2017] UKSC 5

Index

For Product Safety Concerns and Information please contact our EU
representative GPSR@taylorandfrancis.com Taylor & Francis Verlag GmbH,
Kaufingerstraße 24, 80331 München, Germany

Batch number: 08153772

Printed by Printforce, the Netherlands